PROFIT
FIRST
— FOR —
RESTAURANTS

Transform Your Money-Eating Restaurant into a Cash-Making Machine

KASEY ANTON

IngramSpark, La Vergne, TN 37086

ISBN (paperback): 979-8-9873140-1-2
ISBN (ebook): 979-8-9873140-2-9

https://www.kaseyanton.com

Book design by CB Messer

DISCLAIMER: The information contained within this book is for informational purposes only. It should not be considered legal, financial, or tax advice. You should consult with an attorney or tax professional to determine what may be best for your individual needs.

Kasey Anton does not make any guarantee or other promise as to any results that may be obtained from using the content within this book. No one should make any financial decisions without first consulting their own professional team and conducting their own research and due diligence. To the maximum extent permitted by law, Kasey Anton disclaims any and all liability in the event that any information, commentary, analysis, opinions, advice and/ or recommendations herein prove to be inaccurate, incomplete, or unreliable, or result in any investment or other losses.

To protect the privacy of clients and interviewees, some names have been changed.

TESTIMONIALS FOR
PROFIT FIRST FOR RESTAURANTS

"This takes the concepts of *Profit First* and puts them in a way that is relevant to Restaurants. If your restaurant is struggling with cash flow and profitability this book will give you a step-by-step approach to creating profitability in your restaurant. This book stands on its own you do not need to read *Profit First* first in order to get value from this book."

—Ellen Minteer, *Off Your Plate Accounting*

"I would say that this method is a game-changer for how you comprehend and run your business. It is a simple way to understand where your money is at any time. Using it now, I can truly say how remarkable it is and what a positive impact it has had on me. You need to read the book. The idea of sales - profit = expenses makes you think completely differently about running your business. It will make you consider other opportunities within or without your industry. You are confident because you will have mastered making profit from day 1."

—Matt Lombardo, *Sweet Life Catering*

"*Profit First for Restaurants* is a comprehensive view into Cashflow management specific to the challenges all restaurant owners face with covering Payroll, making Profit, and accounting for potential swings in COGS. The book provides real examples of restaurant owners and their journeys."

—Angela Goodman, Founder of Valkyrie Ventures Group, LLC & Owner of Famous Toastery (multiple locations)

"It's a financial system for your restaurant business that takes you out of the 'dream' phase and into a structure that makes your dream sustainable."

—Gena Comenzo, Restaurateur

"*PF for Restaurants* is not only a cash management blueprint for any restaurant owner who wants to run a profitable business, but also it gives you real-world, tactical steps to market, grow, and thrive in an industry that's known for slim to none margins."

—Shawn Vandyke, Author, Business Coach, Entrepreneur

"If you are a robust $50mil+ restaurant company this book probably isn't for you. You already have robust financial systems in place (I hope!). However, this book *is* for those of us that aspire to grow our businesses using our scarce resources as efficiently as possible so that we *can* be the $50mil success story… Practical KISS advice on solid systems for profitability."

—Pete Minich, CEO Fresh City Restaurant Holdings LLC

"Wowza! What an amazing book. I wish I had read this before I started my business. Thankfully I had Ms. Anton as a mentor to help fill in the blanks. I'm not a math whiz by any stretch but the way this book is written and the extremely well thought out graphs and charts are an easy read for even the most business challenged folks like me. Bravo Kasey! This is exactly what every restaurant entrepreneur needs and must read!"

—Tracey Noonan, CEO & Co- Founder Wicked Good Cupcakes, serial entrepreneur, author, and musician

To Clyde and Lucy,
who inspire me every day to become the best version of me.

"HOSPITALITY EXISTS WHEN
YOU BELIEVE THAT THE OTHER
PERSON IS ON YOUR SIDE."

Danny Meyer [1]

CONTENTS

FOREWORD by Mike Michalowicz 1

INTRODUCTION 5

CHAPTER 1: This Is Why I Care 11

    Our Beliefs about the Restaurant Industry 13

    A Better Way 17

    Our Beliefs about the Restaurant Industry **and** Money 19

    A Great Saturday Night Won't Save You 22

    It's Not Just about More Money—The Money Is Already There 26

    You Know How to Hustle 27

CHAPTER 2: This Is Where You Find Out the Money Is Already There ... 31

    Solving Cash Management 33

    GAAP versus Reality 34

    Sales – Expenses = Profit 36

    Sales – **Profit** = Expenses 37

    Parkinson's Law 40

    Bank Balance Accounting 40

    What Is Profit? 43

    A Typical Busy Night: Everything Goes Wrong 44

CHAPTER 3: This Is the Core Cash Management System that Can Save
Your Business 47

    Here's How the System Works 50

    Order Matters! Serve Sequentially 52

    Remove Temptation 57

    It's All about Rhythm 60

    The Five Foundational Accounts (+3) 62

Freaked Out Yet? 63

Profit First Success Story: Bar NYC 66

CHAPTER 4: This Is the Cash Management System on Restaurant
Steroids...69

Introducing MacDaddy PF Cash 69

Meals Tax Account 69

Prime Cost: Payroll Account 70

Prime Cost: COGS (Food and Beverage) Account.................72

If You're Feeling Super Sassy: Advanced Profit First Accounts.............78

Seasonal ("Drip") Account...79

Gift Cards/Certificates Liability Account 83

Delivery Fees 85

Spreadsheets Are NOT the Answer 86

Profit First Success Story: A Small Restaurant Group with Multiple
Owner-Investors...89

CHAPTER 5: This Will Suck, but Do It Anyway 93

Your Instant Assessment 96

Profit First Cautionary Tale: Cassie's Burger Shack 106

CHAPTER 6: This Is How You Will Use the System.................... 113

Charting Your Course to Profit 115

Moving the Money.. 117

Out of Sight, Out of Mind 123

The Story You See.. 129

Profit First Success Story: Prep Kitchen, CA.................... 132

CHAPTER 7: This Is Where Your Restaurant Fits In.................... 135

Understanding and Embracing Your Business Model 139

Here's Why a Business Model Is So Important 140

Figuring Out Your Business Model 141

How to Make Improvements to Move toward
TAPs – GAME PLAN 144

CHAPTER 8: This Is Where We Nail Your Prime Costs 149

Let's Regroup 152

Menu Costing 154

Payroll... 159

CHAPTER 9: This Is Where We Dial in Your Operating Expenses 165

Sometimes the Money Is Hiding in Plain Sight 168

Expense Analysis Exercise 172

Expense Analysis Summary 188

Profit First Success Story: Caterer, Cape Cod 196

CHAPTER 10: This Is Where We Get Straight on Debt 199

Dangerous Debt 203

When You Know You Need to Borrow 205

Another Cautionary Tale: The Tavern 212

CHAPTER 11: This Is Where We Come to Terms with the Fact That

Taxes Are a Thing 217

Tax Lessons from a Non-Tax Person 218

Tax Myths 219

What You Need to Know about Taxes 224

Example: A Restaurateur's Tax Liability 226

Summary 231

Profit First Success Story: A Franchise Story 232

CHAPTER 12: This Is Where Culture Meets Your Bottom Line 239

Culture Is Contagious 243

CHAPTER 13: This Is the Marketing Strategy That Saved My

Restaurant 251

The Marketing Strategy That Saved My Restaurant 253

Marketing That Works 256

Direct Marketing That Works 257

Here's How the Birthday Candle Mailer Worked 259

Quick Staff Training 262

An Easy, Homegrown Database is Money in the Bank 265

What Gets Measured Makes You Money 267

Summary 271

CONCLUSION: And This Is How I Know You Can Do It 273

GLOSSARY OF TERMS 277

ENDNOTES 281

ACKNOWLEDGMENTS... 285

ABOUT THE AUTHOR... 289

MACDADDY RESOURCE MENU 291

READER NOTES..293

FOREWORD

by Mike Michalowicz

GROWING UP IN THE 1970s, my sister and I had a favorite TV show: *Wonder Woman*. Played by Lynda Carter, Wonder Woman defeated evil villains, lassoed the truth from crooks, and was a bullet-deflecting badass as she saved humanity. I was amazed that one person could do so much good.

But as I got older, I became disenchanted. Heroes, it seemed, were pretty much just for the big screen. Sure, the real world had firefighters, soldiers, and such. Those folks are heroes. But heroes for entrepreneurs? Nah. I couldn't imagine anyone fighting for us. And surely there was no hero badass enough to serve the most entrepreneurial of entrepreneurs... restaurateurs.

Not only was no one saving restaurateurs (I thought), the folks who ran restaurants were in an unwinnable battle for their businesses' survival. I knew this because an acclaimed chef and restaurant owner, Mark Tarbell, told me how dire it can be.

I am in a business group of about a hundred entrepreneurs called "Gathering of Titans." Recently, some of the folks in our group had grown and sold their businesses and were seeking to do the "next thing." A popular choice, apparently, is to open a restaurant.

With so many people showing interest in running a restaurant, Mark, a winner of *Iron Chef* and the owner of Tarbell's in Phoenix, Arizona, shared what it takes to own and operate a successful restaurant. I will never forget what he said.

"You can own a restaurant for $100,000," Mark stated.

I could see people lean forward. A few people in our group had started their restaurants for millions and had still failed. Others were struggling and spending a hundred grand a month. So for Mark to start with such a bold statement and seemingly ridiculous number had people intrigued.

Mark continued, "First, pick your favorite restaurant. Then go there at least once a week. Every time you go, tip your waiter a hundred bucks. Tip the host, the captain, the chef, the bartender, the busboy, and the valet one hundred dollars each, too. Do this every week for at least a year. It will cost you around $100,000. Then, at 5:00 p.m. on Valentine's Day, call the restaurant and ask for a 7:00 p.m. seating at the best table in the house. You will get it, flowers on your table and all, because you now 'own' the restaurant."

The group (except for the people who already owned restaurants) laughed at this because of its absurd truth. Many people who start a restaurant do it for bragging rights. They want to show off to their friends. But they surely don't know what they are getting into and are therefore destined to fail.

Other folks go into the business for the right reasons and with the right intent, yet still struggle massively. They know what they are getting into, but they don't know how to manage the ever-changing industry environment (think pandemics, supply chain issues, and the like). Therefore they are destined to fail, too.

The reality is that on the whole, restaurateurs are the poorest of all entrepreneurs. Most are in a fight just to exist, let alone be profitable. Restaurants have countless moving parts, including perishable inventory, unreliable staff, and inconsistent patronage. And most restaurateurs must have a "hustle-or-you-die" mentality to sustain their businesses.

With all the epic challenges restaurateurs face, you surely need a Wonder Woman. And you do. Her name is Kasey Anton.

Kasey is a retired, *successful* restaurant owner who developed countless strategies to make her own restaurant grow profitably and perpetually. Now, she helps other restaurateurs do the same and she has written this book to help you do it, too.

For over fifteen years, Kasey has served restaurateurs as a small business bookkeeper, accountant, and consultant. But what impresses me most is that, during the first half of her life, she worked in every position in multiple types of restaurants. She has done it all in restaurants, including owning one, and her work has culminated in serving you. She is devoted to making the entire restaurant industry fiscally strong and permanently profitable. After all, the only business that can truly serve you is one that is truly financially stable. Profit matters. A lot.

There is so much more I could share with you about Kasey and Profit First, but I fear that would only delay you getting the information you need most. In this book, you will find the solution to your financial troubles. I don't say that flippantly. Profit First has been deployed by over 700,000 companies.

Now, Kasey will show you how to do it with yours. But before I depart, I have one final story to share…

I have had dozens of videoconferencing calls with Kasey, but I only noticed recently that there is a painting of Wonder Woman on her wall. When I commented on how much I loved that show as a kid and how badass Wonder Woman was, Kasey looked at the painting over her shoulder, then back at me, and said, "Yeah, she is my hero. I want to be just like her."

Guess what, Kasey. You are.

—Mike Michalowicz

INTRODUCTION

WE HAVE A RUNNING JOKE in my office. Whenever a potential client comes in to discuss their new business idea, I say to my team, "How quickly do you think I can talk them out of this?"

Why? Because businesses fail. A lot. And restaurants? Restaurants come and go and have one of the highest failure rates of any industry. If you've been around the industry for any amount of time, I'm sure you've heard this. It's no secret. And yet aspiring restaurateurs still dare to start these businesses, logic and common sense be damned.

People don't open restaurants just because they want to start a business if they did, they'd choose one with a much better success rate. People open restaurants because they are building a dream. And while I may try to talk people out of their business ideas all day long, I know I can't talk you out of it.

You're a restaurateur. You're a different breed.

But I wish I could talk you out of it. Because while you have the passion, the skills, and—God knows—the work ethic to pull it off, the thing that kills the dream every time is money. And it's not just the lack of money, it's the lack of profit. That is what causes you to struggle and kills the dream.

I have been in the restaurant industry for decades. I have worked in all kinds of restaurants. I have worked in every position. I have started restaurants and I have sold them. And now I save them.

For the past fifteen years, I have been in and out of hundreds, possibly even thousands of businesses, many of them restaurants, and from my behind-the-scenes financial viewpoint, it's not pretty. Because it doesn't matter if you're the world's greatest chef or manager, have a concept that will knock people's socks off, or found the location to beat all locations; none of those things equate to having a successful business. As the saying goes, "The last thing you need to know how to do to open a restaurant is cook."

Having culinary, hospitality, and people-management skills is only half the battle. Maybe even less than half. The other half, the other extremely important skill to have, is money management. And with everything I have seen and experienced, I strongly believe that money management is the most important skill a successful business owner can have. Money stays away from people who can't manage it.

Believe it or not, there is a simple fix for this problem, and it's called MacDaddy PF Cash. (Later on in this book, you'll learn why I gave it that name.) This is a cash management system based on Profit First, the proven approach detailed in the bestselling book *Profit First* by Mike Michalowicz.[2] I designed MacDaddy PF Cash specifically for restaurants, with your unique needs, challenges, and requirements in mind. This custom system instills permanent profitability in your restaurant. And if you think profitability is not a top priority, think again. Profitability is the *only* way a business can survive. Not many people realize that, which is why so many businesses fail.

I once had a very "successful" restaurant—or so I thought—until it wasn't successful anymore, and we were forced to either sell or go down with the ship. And I can tell you with candor and complete confidence that the outcome would have been quite different had this book existed back when I was running my restaurant. There is no doubt in my mind about that. But this book did *not* exist. The closure of my restaurant took me down a different path—a path that led me to write this book, for you, so that you can have a different outcome.

Look, I don't know if you're going to read this thing. I know how busy you are. With that in mind, I wrote it as simply as I could and with the easiest how-to instructions I could create. I even designed tools you can use to make implementing MacDaddy PF Cash and creating a profitable business even easier.

Throughout this book, I share some of the many success stories of restaurants we have helped, even transformed, over the years. I share my own story. And I know with every fiber of my being that this book will help your restaurant, too. It may even save it.

So please, read it. Read it between shifts, or first thing in the morning, or at the end of service, or on your day off. Or download the audiobook and listen to it in the car or on the train, while you're at the gym or out for a quick walk, or as you chop vegetables or polish glasses. And if your restaurant is not on the road to permanent profitability by the time you finish reading this book, I want to know. Or if you just hate it, I want to know. But if you like it, if it speaks to you, if it helps you in any way, if it brings you hope and joy or even just a smile and a nod, I want to know that too. This is my life's work. And what gives it meaning is being able to share what I have learned so others can continue to do great things and build their dreams.

You don't have to struggle to make it in the restaurant business. If you want to build a restaurant where the money is managed, cash is flowing, profit is priority, and your dream is the reality, this is the book for you.

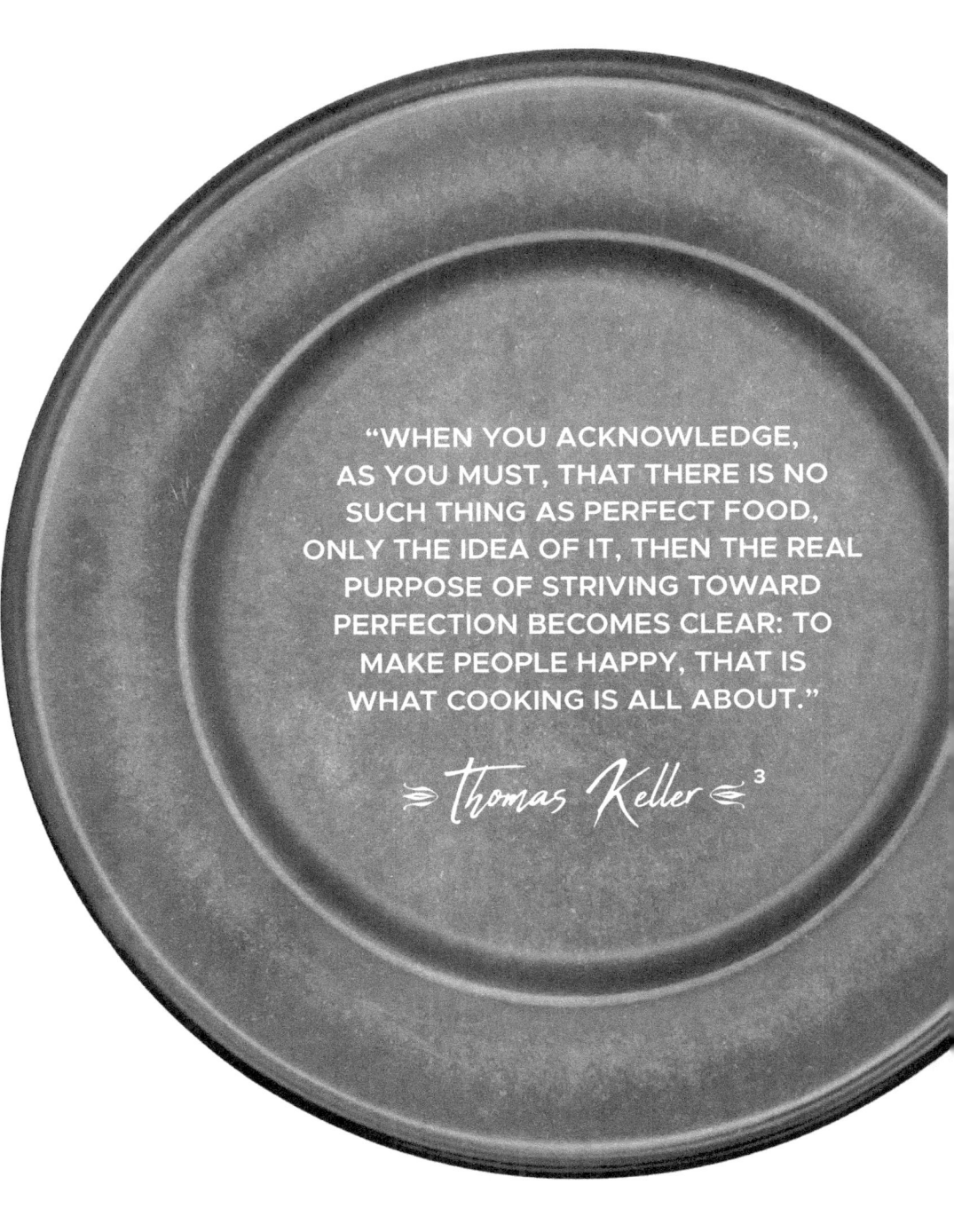

"WHEN YOU ACKNOWLEDGE, AS YOU MUST, THAT THERE IS NO SUCH THING AS PERFECT FOOD, ONLY THE IDEA OF IT, THEN THE REAL PURPOSE OF STRIVING TOWARD PERFECTION BECOMES CLEAR: TO MAKE PEOPLE HAPPY, THAT IS WHAT COOKING IS ALL ABOUT."

Thomas Keller [3]

CHAPTER 1

This Is Why I Care

"It's not hearts and lungs, people. It's just dinner."

This may go down as one of my staff's greatest comments. Someone shouted it out during an incredibly busy Saturday night, when the stress level was peaking and the chef was about to blow a gasket, but the statement was not meant to minimize or trivialize the work that was being performed that night in any way. Far from it. As a former restaurateur, current consultant, and long-time enthusiast, I believe that the work performed in restaurants across the world is some of the most important, meaningful, and significant work of our time—of any time. Because this work we do is based in joy: celebrations of achievement, relationships, self-care, and even lifelong memories.

Given that the work of restaurants is so vital, it seems almost ironic that our industry "suffers" more than most. The COVID-19 pandemic notwithstanding, most small business restaurants (so, maybe not McDonald's) have an incredibly hard time staying alive, let alone operating at a profit. On top of that, the work can at times be grueling (extremely hot kitchens, all kinds of equipment malfunctions, fire, broken glass, sharp knives, not-the-most-reliable part-time staff, and drunken patrons) and the industry in general has a century-long reputation for being extremely demanding. Restaurants are living, breathing entities; even if they close for a day, there are no days off for their owners.

An industry whose primary purpose is to facilitate joy and celebration is also one of the most stressful and least profitable of all industries? That can't be right. And yet it is.

Much like a seasonal business in which, for example, landscapers need to make their money during a short season, for restaurants, the "short season" is the weekend—more specifically, Saturday night. Somewhere along the way, Saturday night became the bar that was set for "success." That is when the restaurant is operating at capacity and fully staffed, reservations are sold out, the kitchen bustles all day with deliveries and prep staff, pre-shift meetings are mandatory, and the buzz in the air is unlike the energy at any other job you may have had. As I write this paragraph, I can almost feel what it's like to prepare for a big night. This is our Super Bowl. But it doesn't happen once a year. It happens every Saturday night.

Exciting stuff, right? It is! Except it comes with some baggage. If this is where we set the bar, then any other night that doesn't measure up is a failure. Once we know what our restaurant is capable of, we want that all the time. Who wouldn't? There are few restaurants (and I mean very few) that frequently operate at capacity. Some have several Saturdays each week, not just one, but these are the unicorns and—just like real unicorns—you don't see a lot of them. But this is where we set the bar, so we keep going after it. The problem is, when we set our expectations too high and can't achieve them, frustration ensues. We start looking in all the wrong places to solve this problem.

Constantly trying to solve the problem that every night isn't Saturday night is costing you more than you may realize.

Maybe you recognize some of these "solutions":

"It must be the menu!" Changing menu items is costly both in time and money and lacks consistency, so that doesn't help.

"We need more advertising!" Advertising can get very expensive, is difficult to measure in terms of effectiveness, and almost never helps.

"Maybe it's the prices, or the color of the walls, or the concept itself!" Again, these changes can be expensive and time-consuming. And they come with no guarantees.

Maybe you have tried one or all of these solutions. Or maybe you just keep doing what you're doing, week in and week out, while secretly (or not-so-secretly) praying for another Saturday night. And when that doesn't happen, you hang your head, review your options, realize you don't have the time or the money to execute any of the options, and go back to doing what you've always done: hope and pray for another Saturday night. Repeat.

This struggle is real. So why do we do it?

OUR BELIEFS ABOUT THE RESTAURANT INDUSTRY

When I was little, and as far back as I can remember, all I wanted to do was own a restaurant.

Occasionally, my parents took me and my two older brothers out to dinner at Lum's, a small family restaurant located in the only strip mall in Old Saybrook, Connecticut, at the time. I remember the dark wood tables and chairs, the worn red carpet, and the smell. God, how I loved that smell. To me, it smelled like happiness from the moment I stepped through the door. The aroma wrapped me up and transported me to a place where my family could all sit at the same table and not get yelled at for being picky eaters or just being idiots. We could order whatever we wanted off the children's menu, which was filled with possibilities: hamburgers, chicken fingers, french fries, all the things I loved and none of the homemade "healthy" stuff I hated.

And that aroma? Come to find out years later, that magical scent was grease. And you know what? I don't even care. I loved it then and I still love it now. Grease is the word, as they say.

Even at a young age, I knew that eating out every night was unrealistic; my parents constantly reminded us that money doesn't grow on trees. But all I wanted to do was recreate that experience of eating at a restaurant as often as possible. And I am not talking about pouring cereal into bowls, either; once a week, almost every week for years, I set our rarely-used dining room table and cooked a three- or four-course dinner just for my parents that was ready when they got home from work. I was the hostess, waitress, prep cook, and chef. I'd pour them water, serve them bread, cook the food (with a little help from my mom) and plate it up as prettily as I could. And because I was so thoughtful and ambitious in designing these "restaurant at home" nights, I rarely had to be the dishwasher. We left that to my brother Matt.

I vividly recall making stuffed mushrooms for an appetizer one night, followed by a garden salad. I believe I also made Chicken Kiev and rice pilaf for the main course, with brownie sundaes for dessert. Don't get too excited—the Chicken Kiev came frozen and fully cooked and it's hard to screw up a box of Rice-a-Roni, but I heated those up like a champ.

I was an ambitious ten-year-old. I knew what I wanted and was going after it. And I think my parents enjoyed those nights overall; not all my dishes were winners, but in the end, they didn't have to cook. Even with all that youthful chutzpah, though, my parents begged me not to go into the restaurant industry. Neither of them had ever worked in hospitality, but even they had heard the stories. They would say, "It's a grueling business," and while it was fine for a part-time job while I was in school, they made it very clear that they did not want me to make a career out of it. My dad would tell me the failure rate of restaurants—"Fifty percent!"—and that I'd be better off with a more "professional" career choice.

I started working in restaurants as a dishwasher at Bonanza when I was fourteen. Though my passion for the restaurant industry had not wavered, my parents felt the same about hospitality when it was time to look at colleges. "It's too narrow a path," they would say, and I honestly believe they thought I would grow out of this phase.

Out of respect for my parents, and adhering to their words of caution, I did not go to college to study hospitality. I went to the University of Rhode Island, where I studied communications and business. And what did I do when I graduated? I got a job at the Chart House Restaurant and, a year later, I entered their industry-renowned management training program, "CHAMP" (which stood for "Chart House Administrative Management Program").

From a very early age, I was taught that a career in the restaurant industry was an undesirable path and would lead to a life of struggle. And you know what? My parents may have been right.

We all have our Lum's, and our dreams and stories from childhood. We have also absorbed early messages that formed our belief that the restaurant industry is hard. And because this is what we've been told, we're not surprised when it is. While we may complain about working doubles, pulling eighteen-hour shifts, and working seven days a week including all holidays and weekends, we think it's just the way it is.

There is a belief within the industry that working in a restaurant is a daily battle. There are always a million things happening and a zillion moving parts, which means about a trillion things that can, and often do, go wrong. This is the norm. A constant head-butt against a brick wall.

Take a moment to think about the restaurant bosses you've had. Chances are, they weren't the happiest people you've ever met. When I think back to all my bosses—from those early days at Bonanza to the Steak Loft in Mystic, Connecticut to the Chart House in Boston and many, many places in between—the word "happy" is not one I would necessarily use to describe many of them. "Stressed," "overwhelmed," "on edge," and "unhappy" better describe their state most of the time. This is certainly true of the chefs I've worked with. What started out as a fun or exciting buildup to a busy night ahead almost always ended with screaming, yelling, F-bombs and insults flying, finger-pointing, and tears being shed, usually less than halfway through the night. "You gotta have thick skin to work in this business" was often used as an excuse for this behavior.

Why do we allow it? Because it's what we were taught to expect. It's part of our belief system about how a restaurant is *supposed* to function. It's supposed to be hard. We believe it's the cost of entry. The cost of experiencing the kind of energy and excitement you don't get to experience in other jobs. And this is the status quo.

But it doesn't have to be.

A BETTER WAY

There's always a better way. While the restaurant industry is flooded with overworked and overstressed managers and owners, there is always that one exception to the rule. Mine came in the form of Todd. He was a dining room manager for the Chart House in Boston when I first started there. He hadn't been there long, but boy did he stand out. Why? Because he was always smiling. He was always happy! Nothing could bring this dude down. Todd was great at his job, and everyone wanted to work on his shifts. And this wasn't because he had the best shifts or because he was great at filling out end-of-night paperwork. It's because he was a pleasure to be around.

As a manager, Todd set the tone. He knew what most of us easily forgot: that we were serving dinner, not solving the problem of world peace; that our guests were there for a joyful evening; and that our job was to ensure that happened. Period. Case closed. If we could get on board with that, if we could focus on providing a wonderful dining experience, then we could all be on the same page and ensure a smooth night ahead with no reason for screaming, yelling, F-bombs and insults flying, finger-pointing, or tears being shed. We could all participate in the joy.

I vividly recall one evening when things were beginning to heat up, the restaurant was filling quickly, and the kitchen was humming. I needed Todd's help. I don't remember exactly what the issue was, but I do recall feeling anxious as I approached him about whatever problem I was having.

"Todd," I said nervously, "I have a question…"

Before I could finish my sentence, Todd smiled and said, "Well, Kasey, I have the answer."

This simple reply shifted everything for me that night, and for many nights to come. It reminded me that no matter what was going on or what I was about to ask, there was a simple enough solution. We, after all, were serving dinner! It taught me that getting stressed out wasn't going to help anything or anyone. Quite the reverse.

And while it wasn't Todd who shouted out, "It's not hearts and lungs, people, it's just dinner"—that happened many years later—he innately knew this to be true. Which is why the shifts he ran were the most popular, the most fun, the least stressful, and provided the best guest experiences. Win, win, win. And while I was not involved with the finances of the Chart House at the time, I have no doubt that these nights were not only successful from an overall-experience viewpoint, but also from a financial one.

OUR BELIEFS ABOUT THE RESTAURANT INDUSTRY *AND* MONEY

NOT ONLY DO WE PILE on the pressure through our belief that we must recreate Saturday every night of the week, and that it will be a hard and painful process; we also believe we have to struggle with the money. After all, if we set the bar at a Saturday night of sales, anything less is failure. Which means we will always come up short: short on getting the vendors paid on time, short on ordering the supplies we need or late getting the equipment fixed, possibly short on payroll (eek), and definitely short on paying ourselves and profit. We will always struggle to pay our bills and meet our obligations on time. We have accepted this as the norm and do nothing about it because it is considered the fate of a restaurateur.

One of the many problems with that is, the rest of the world thinks we're loaded. How many requests do you get each year to donate a dinner for two to some random club you've never heard of because "it'll be great advertising"? Translation: "You're a restaurant. You make tons of money."

Right?

There's no money. And if you really think about it, it kind of makes sense that there is no money.

Look at it this way: There is only so much you can charge for a steak.

Consider the math. A decent steak may cost a restaurant fifteen dollars to purchase.

If you own a nice steakhouse, you might be able to charge forty-five dollars for that steak.

That's a thirty-dollar profit, right?

Nope.

Because that "profit" doesn't include paying the chef who grilled the steak. Or the kitchen manager who ordered and received it. Or the prep cook who prepared the grill station. Nor does it include what you pay the dishwasher to clean not only the dish the steak was served on, but the glasses, the silverware, the grill, the entire kitchen, and oftentimes the restaurant as well. It doesn't include what the waitstaff, bussers, food runners, bartenders, bar backs, valets, hosts, assistant managers, dining room managers, sommeliers, or general manager get paid. And it certainly doesn't include the cost of rent, utilities, linen, insurances (and there are many), menus, computer "stuff," dues, licenses, office supplies, dishes, silverware, glasses, to-go boxes, to-go anything, advertising, marketing, credit card fees—I could go on and on, but you get me.

Know what else it doesn't include? The complimentary bread and butter you provide at the beginning of the meal. Or the candle, the salt and pepper, or any other condiment.

The result? To make a buck, you'd better sell a lot of steaks. And I mean a *lot*.

Some places do just that! Even if you're not a steak person, you may have heard of Ruth's Chris, Morton's of Chicago, The Capital Grille, even the 99 Restaurant (though whether we can call that a steakhouse is debatable). These places sell a lot of steak. I am guessing that the owners of these restaurants are not reading this book. That's not to say they shouldn't! But if you're selling enough steaks to pay your bills and have something left over, that's winning the lottery by restaurant standards.

Unfortunately, most restaurants, especially the smaller, independent restaurants that I serve, do not sell quite as many steaks. If they're "lucky," they might sell a good amount on a Saturday night. That Saturday night might be profitable on its own, but it's not on its own. That Saturday night needs to feed Sunday, Monday, Tuesday, Wednesday, Thursday, and maybe even Friday night, when too few steaks are sold to pay the bills, much less turn a profit.

This formula of waiting, hoping, and praying for fortune like that of the steakhouses I mentioned above—that every night of the week will turn into a Saturday night—creates an environment, a culture of constant weekly, cyclical struggle. And this place, this pattern of living for another Saturday night, keeps *you* in a state of constant struggle.

It's the wrong mindset.

You don't need to keep looking for another Saturday night. As a matter of fact, the sheer act of searching for this rare unicorn is what is holding you back.

Your struggle affects everyone and everything. The emotional and financial stress that you consistently suffer affect every component of your business. And ultimately, they affect your bottom line.

You don't have to struggle to make it in the restaurant business.

The money is already there.

It's just not being managed.

Here's what I know. The restaurant industry has more moving parts than your average industry. A restaurant's P&L (profit and loss report, also known as an income statement, which tracks sales and expenses) is longer because there's more stuff to keep track of. The restaurant industry, especially when it comes to the smaller, independent restaurants, is one of nickels and dimes. This means you need to watch every penny. The margins are tight. There's a lot to look at and control. An average small business might have a one- or two-page P&L and three or four KPIs (key performance indicators). A restaurant might have a four- or five-page P&L and about twelve KPIs.

Bottom line, there's a ton to know, tweak, fix, and stay on top of. Strangely enough, managing the money from the moment it hits your account has not traditionally been one of those things. Restaurants are always playing defense, waiting for that Saturday night to hit so that when those funds drop into the account the following Monday or Tuesday, bills can be paid, payroll can run, and the lights can stay on for another day. And then they stress out for the rest of the week, waiting for Saturday to come so they can do this dance all over again. Week after week.

This has become the norm.

A GREAT SATURDAY NIGHT WON'T SAVE YOU

Sometimes, Saturday is not even Saturday anymore.

When my partners and I opened Bomboa Restaurant in Boston's Back Bay in November 1999, it was the best of times.

It was all that was right in the restaurant world. We had many Saturday nights each week, high energy, high sales, the who's who of the Boston restaurant scene dining with us, and articles written about us and our success. We were riding high and loving every minute of it, often traveling to New York City to check out the new and exciting restaurants and chefs popping up and garnering lots of media attention. Our chef from Bomboa was invited to cook at the acclaimed James Beard House, and of course we made a long weekend of it and expensed everything through our restaurant as it was a "business trip."

We bought fancy new chairs, fancy plates, and fancy lights. We even tried fancy uniforms for a while (that didn't last, and I don't recommend it) because the money was flowing in. It flowed out just as quickly as it came in, but that didn't really matter because we could count on a good three or four Saturdays every week.

Until it did matter.

On September 11, 2001, the world came to a screeching halt.

I cannot even begin to describe how that day changed the lives of so many, way beyond how it changed life for me and my restaurant at the time. I cannot even begin to imagine what it was like to be a New Yorker or to have lost a loved one on that day. That heartbreak is paralyzing. I get chills every time I think back to that day, that moment when our world and our worldviews changed forever. I am not going to write about the events of that day; I could never do them justice. But what I do want to tell you about is how everything changed in the restaurant world.

My partners and I went from the best of times to the worst of times.

For quite a while after what we now call 9/11, the dining scene was nearly nonexistent. Not only was there no travel, but also, people held few celebrations at that time or for months afterward. And when our world, our lives, some "normalcy" started to slowly come back, diners chose comfort over anything "exotic" and to stay closer to home. Gone were the days of dining out to see and be seen, or as theater. There was a definite shift in the dining world toward more connection. Diners weren't seeking to be entertained anymore, they simply wanted time with their loved ones. And they could do that closer to home, or even in their own homes.

I felt the same way. So, when sales went from nonexistent to barely a trickle as the world began to open up again, we realized that we were in trouble. We had built our restaurant to live off multiple Saturday nights each week, and when we couldn't produce even one Saturday night, we had nothing but problems.

At times, we struggled to pay our vendors so we could get food, beverages, and other items delivered in anticipation of a busy weekend. And boy, did we need that weekend. We depended on busy weekends to keep us going. I remember fretting about whether we could cover payroll. I even remember a few times when we had to ask some employees to hold their paychecks a few extra days so they wouldn't bounce. And I will never forget the Saturday night when all the toilets backed up and flooded the kitchen, but we refused to close the restaurant because *it was Saturday night and we needed it.* We trudged through that night for as long as we could, but when the chef was standing in about a foot of sewage while plating main courses for a party of ten, we knew we had taken it too far. And although we did finish serving that table of ten, we closed the kitchen right afterward.

The next day was Sunday in Boston, when pretty much nothing is open and no one is working. But there I was, with my business partners and the yellow pages (this was before most businesses had websites), searching for an emergency plumbing company that would come out and dig up a street in downtown Boston to fix the broken sewer pipe—*on a Sunday*. We were desperate. We could not afford to be closed one night, let alone the number of nights we feared we might have to close to get it fixed.

I think I was on my sixth or seventh call when a young man answered. He was home "on his couch" —because it was Sunday—and I begged him to help us, promising him free food and beers for probably a lifetime. Sure enough, he had access to an excavator and called some buddies, and they came and fixed the pipe so we could open the next day.

For the next five years, we struggled and then struggled some more. We took on expensive debt to pay bills and make payroll. We cut every corner possible on every expense we could and thought nobody noticed. (They did, but it would be years before we realized this.)

How did we go from making money hand over fist for the first couple of years in business to not having two nickels to rub together, literally overnight?

The truth was that the money was there. We just hadn't managed it properly.

IT'S NOT JUST ABOUT MORE MONEY—THE MONEY IS ALREADY THERE

IT WAS MANY YEARS LATER—AFTER we sold the restaurant and I'd had my first kid and started a small bookkeeping and consulting business—that I had my epiphany about money management.

I was on my honeymoon when I first read *Profit First*. It was either the first or second day, and I was sitting outside on a white chaise lounge on an expansive, beautiful emerald-green lawn overlooking the Atlantic Ocean in Ogunquit, Maine. The book had been recommended to me a few times over the years, and I had finally decided to check it out. My business, Spark Business Consulting, was growing strong, yet I struggled to get my clients to listen to me. I thought maybe *Profit First* would give me some ideas about how to help them understand the money in their businesses.

Two chapters in, I knew immediately that this system could help so many businesses. I knew this because my company works with hundreds of small businesses that all suffer from the same problem—cash mismanagement. By the third chapter, I was transported back to my restaurant days. It had been more than ten years since I'd sold Bomboa, in 2006. I thought, *Oh my God, we weren't managing the cash right!* It wasn't the menu, or the staff, or 9/11, or the concept. If we had just managed our cash properly, we would have been able to weather any disruption and manage our day-to-day challenges. Saturday night wouldn't have been make-or-break, *it would just be dinner.*

If I had this book back then, I thought, *I might still have my restaurant. Or a different restaurant. Or a chain of restaurants.* The worst of times would have become the best of times. I knew it in my bones: I had just found the Holy Grail of "lifeblood" (cash flow) for small businesses.

I recall leaping off my chaise and running back into our hotel room to grab my phone and call the number listed in the book to become a Profit First Professional. And the rest, as they say, is history.

YOU KNOW HOW TO HUSTLE

You aren't a typical small business owner. You are a restaurateur. You understand the hustle it takes to get things done in this industry. It's never pretty. Over my years working with hundreds of small businesses, I haven't seen that kind of hustle in other industries very often. I'm not sure that non-restaurateurs know it exists. I believe that most business owners would call the landlord and go home if their toilets flooded. Enjoy the day off. Have zero stress. It doesn't work that way in the restaurant business. "You hustle or you die" was the business lesson of my lifetime.

Until Profit First came along.

My biggest success to date by far is Profit First. Implementing and running this system within my business, watching what it does and how it helps to orchestrate my decision-making, has been monumentally important for the success and prosperity of my company. While I knew it would work from the outset, I had no idea what tremendous growth we would undergo because of it. I attribute not just the growth of my company, but the growth of my personal and financial success to Profit First as well.

When clients ask me, "What's so great about Profit First?" or "Why does it work so well?" my first answer is that when you put intention behind just about anything, you get results. It's as simple as that. If you set an intention to go to the gym every morning and do it, you will see physical results. If you set an intention to eat healthier and consume fewer calories, you will lose weight. If you set an intention to read more, you will read more books. And when you set an intention for every dollar that comes into your business and follow through with that intention, magic happens. Except it's not really magic, it's common sense and logic. Which is why it works.

You're a restaurateur; you're no stranger to hard work. You know how to hustle. And implementing Profit First is the endeavor that will change everything.

Every business has *something*, some uphill battle. Everyone has something to complain about, and legitimately so! Do restaurant owners have more to complain about than most? Maybe. Probably. But that doesn't have to equate to a lack of money and constant stress. There's a better way, and I am going to share that with you in this book.

You don't have to struggle to make it in the restaurant business. It can be joyful. It can be what you dreamt about. It can be the best of Saturday night, people, celebrations, laughter, feeling excited, having fun, and great food.

By the end of this book, you will have a cash management system in place that will help you stop worrying about money and get back to the pure joy of hospitality.

CHAPTER 2

This Is Where You Find Out the Money Is Already There

THE MONEY WE NEED TO run our restaurants, pay our bills, pay our people, and pay ourselves is already there. We just haven't managed it correctly. And because we haven't managed it correctly, or maybe even at all, our revenue hasn't been able to support us in the way we need it to. What happens is, we work our fingers to the bone to get to that Saturday night, and when the money comes in, we spend it. All of it. Because we *believe* we must; not only have we been conditioned to accept that this industry is hard and grueling, we have also learned along the way that unless we have multiple Saturday nights each week, there's just not enough money. Which is why we work our fingers to the bone. To get to those Saturdays, to spend the money that we earn, and then do it all over again, week after week.

What we don't do is stop long enough, or with intention and purpose, to look at the money we already have before we spend it. We're just always looking for more. Our belief that there is never enough leads us to constantly pursue that Saturday night "windfall" rather than look at the money we already have and use it intentionally. This is the difference between the stress of needing every night to be Saturday and the calm of simply feeling in control of your business.

So what if we change the story, the narrative, the beliefs that we have held since this industry first captured our hearts? What if we can recapture that early joy, take a breath, smile, and remember why we do what we do? What if we can be more like Todd, the restaurant manager with every answer and an easy smile? He understood and embraced that above all else, we're here to serve dinner and make people happy.

And, what if we choose to manage the money differently?

Parkinson's Law, named after the author and historian C. Northcote Parkinson, teaches us that "work" will expand or contract to match the time given for the task.[4] The same is true of money. If someone hands you ten dollars and tells you to buy groceries to create a three-course dinner for two, what happens? You get *really* innovative with that menu design and most likely come up with something creative and phenomenal. If someone hands you a hundred dollars for the same task, what happens? I'm sure the menu is great; maybe you even serve filet mignon. But given that kind of budget, you may not need to put a ton of thought or innovation into it. In both situations, you have some money, you buy some stuff to complete a task, and you make it work. Other than the amount of money in your budget, what is the real difference between these two scenarios? The difference is the intention. With ten dollars, you have to give every dollar—every dime, really—a very specific task in order to execute a well-crafted three-course dinner. With one hundred dollars, the sky's the limit.

The money was always there. You just managed it differently.

I'll tell you what. If you choose to manage money as I lay it out for you in this book, you will experience some eye-opening, life-altering changes. You will set up guardrails around your money; you will give it a specific purpose; and, possibly for the first time, you will be in the driver's seat and know exactly where you're headed and how to get there—no matter what happens on Saturday night.

SOLVING CASH MANAGEMENT

THERE ARE TWO WAYS TO solve the cash management problem in any restaurant.

1. Sell out the restaurant two-and-a-half to three turns every night of the week with near-perfect prime costs, on-point operational costs, in-line occupancy costs, and a chunky bottom line. Did I mention that you need to do this every day?
2. Put intention behind every dollar and implement a simple cash management system that works.

If item number one describes your restaurant, congratulations! You are a rare unicorn and, some would say, very lucky. However, you can probably (and by probably, I mean definitely) still benefit from a system that manages all that wonderful incoming cash; that institutes and promotes permanent and maximum profitability; and that creates incredible efficiencies, among other wonderful traits.

If your restaurant does run according to item number one, then you may not be reading this book (although you should). But what you will learn in this book will absolutely solve for restaurants that fall under the second category, and the benefits are vast and innumerable.

To get started, let's do a tiny, basic accounting lesson. You're going to love it.

GAAP VERSUS REALITY

So, there's this thing called GAAP. You may or may not have heard of it. It stands for "generally accepted accounting principles." These are the universal accounting rules followed in the US. They tell us what assets and liabilities are versus income and expenses, boring stuff like that. GAAP is a set of rules that we follow without question. Why? Well, it makes logical sense. All the pieces fit together like a nice puzzle and everything balances, just the way accountants like it.

So why question it?

Because whoever came up with GAAP clearly didn't run a restaurant where, chances are, the person or people controlling the numbers, the money, are not actually logical. At least not all the time, and certainly not about money.

One of my favorite quotes from *Profit First* is, "GAAP is meant for logical beings who plan ahead and who never have cash flow problems."[5] Sound like you? I didn't think so.

If you are like so many others (basically everyone) when it comes to bookkeeping, either you, your bookkeeper, or your accountant are following GAAP like a champ. You are recording sales, paying meals tax, entering payroll, paying bills, etc. And at the end of it all, you cross your fingers, make a wish, and hope there's something left over to pay yourself. Or get that new oven or refrigerator. Or get caught up with vendors. Or buy new glassware or paint the bathrooms.

If you're in really rough shape, there may be times when you just pray you can meet payroll or—and this can be the kiss of death—get caught up on back taxes (yikes). And then, of course, there is the obligatory monthly meeting where you review the prior month's P&L (profit and loss report) and either hang your head in shame at the dismal state of your numbers or pat yourself on the back for a job well done.

"Well done" could mean that you hit all your prime-cost targets, kept overhead under control, and possibly show a nice, juicy bottom line. The problem is, this bottom line is a number on a piece of paper, or the computer screen, that quite literally has squat to do with how much money you have in the bank that day or whether you can pay your bills, and it shows a profit amount that is virtually meaningless. If your profit isn't actual cash money in a bank account that you can point to and say, "There's my profit!" then it ain't real profit. Or at least, it isn't profit that you can do anything with, such as pay down debt or investments, reward the owner, or invest in equipment or growth. As a matter of fact, the only thing you can do with "paper profit" is pay taxes on it (more on that in a later chapter). If I had a dime for every time a restaurateur said to me, "It's a mystery to me, where all the money goes!" or "I just don't know why I never have enough money in the bank," or "It goes out faster than it comes in," I'd have a lot of dimes. More than enough to buy out your restaurant two-and-a-half to three times a night and "solve" all your problems—except that wouldn't solve all your problems.

Here's the thing—where the money goes isn't a mystery at all. I'll explain.

Whether you believe it or not, or are conscious of it or not, you put intention behind every dollar you spend. The problem is, and the above-mentioned money confusion ensues, when you are unaware of the intention you are putting behind your dollars. In addition, and even worse, is that you are probably following the traditional GAAP accounting formula we have all been taught:

Sales – Expenses = Profit.

SALES – EXPENSES = PROFIT

THIS FORMULA IS A PROBLEM. While logically and mathematically sound, it works against our human nature. It most certainly works against the average restaurateur's nature. What this equation really tells us is to grab as much in sales as we can (which is why "sales" is in the first position in this formula), pay all the necessary bills, and then call whatever is left over "profit" (which is in last place). The way this equation reads, and the way our brains see it, takes all the energy and importance from profit and leaves it last, unimportant, an afterthought.

Thinking this way is detrimental to our businesses. It takes all the focus from profit and places it squarely on the shoulders of sales and expenses, thus creating the cycle that every restaurant ends up in: waiting for that Saturday night (sales) so that we can pay all our bills (expenses).

Sales and expenses may rise and fall together; but if we're keeping it real, the truth is that while expenses increase when sales do, they do not decrease as quickly as sales do, if at all. And this is where you get stuck in the never-ending, self-defeating cycle of chasing every Saturday night.

SALES – PROFIT = EXPENSES

IF WE CHANGE UP THAT traditional equation, truly amazing things can happen. Let's try it.

$$\text{Sales} - \textbf{Profit} = \text{Expenses}.$$

I don't know about you, but I just felt the earth move a little bit. I mean, with the Profit First formula, the math stays the same and GAAP is still in check, meaning we aren't breaking any accounting laws or creating more work for our CPAs, but the areas of focus shift massively. Now, sales and profit share the spotlight and the expenses are the afterthought.

Let's think on this. Imagine you're sitting in your Accounting 101 class in high school, taking notes and learning all about how businesses work. The teacher is up at the blackboard, the interactive whiteboard, or whatever they use to teach these days, and they write this formula on it: "Sales – Profit = Expenses." And then they tell you that in the business world, you start with sales, and then take the profit, and whatever is left over is used for expenses. They go on to tell you that profit is essential to any business. Not only does it serve many functions, but by taking it first and thereby making it a priority, you ensure the success of that business. These are basic facts.

Now, if we had never been taught the GAAP equation "Sales – Expenses = Profit," then this lecture would not seem that exciting. We would simply take "Sales – Profit = Expenses" as truth, write it in our notes, and hopefully get it right on the final exam. And then we would take this knowledge out into the world and use it in our own businesses and those we manage.

If the "Sales – Profit = Expenses" Profit First formula were the norm, the failure rate of businesses—of restaurants—would be staggeringly low, because businesses would automatically be profitable. And profit is required for a business to grow, let alone survive. We would understand from the outset that profit is a choice, and we would make that choice every day. Our businesses would thrive.

"What about the expenses?" you ask. "Every business has expenses!" Yes, they do, and when you use the Profit First equation, your expenses fall in line with what the business can afford. Instead of allowing the business to incur all of the expenses that you somehow deem to be important at the time you incur them (or think you can afford because you look at the balance in your bank account and assume that's what you can spend), you are forced to operate within the guardrails of what is left over after profit.

This is not to say that you'll take 95% profit and leave 5% for your expenses. While that sounds amazing, I have yet to run into a business with a 95% profit margin. (That would be a unicorn with golden wings and diamond shoes.) Most businesses run somewhere between a 5% and 20% profit margin. Most of your revenue will be used for expenses, just not *all* of it. When you take your profit first and let the leftovers fund the expenses, you build a business that is a lean, mean, money-making machine.

Okay, I know, I can sense your eyes rolling after you just read that. And now I can read your mind:

"Easier said than done."

"Duh, if I could have fewer expenses, don't you think I would?"

"You don't understand how expensive it is to run a restaurant."

Am I right? Close?

Let me address these responses quickly here.

"Easier said than done." True. I cannot necessarily say that implementing Profit First will be easy. It might not be. But I *can* tell you that it is simple. And the benefits far, far outweigh any hardship you may experience during implementation.

"Duh, if I could have fewer expenses, don't you think I would?" Nope. Not if you don't know any better and keep spending every penny you have.

"You don't understand how expensive it is to run a restaurant." Yes, I do. As I mentioned previously, managing others' restaurants and my own is all I knew for more than twenty-five years. And over the last fifteen years, I've helped more than seventy restaurants and hundreds of other businesses with exactly this issue of money management. I understand more than most. I have lived and breathed it. And because I have walked in your shoes, fought the same battles, and share the same cynicism, let me offer some proof that what I am going to teach you is going to work.

PARKINSON'S LAW

As I said earlier, the universal truth known as Parkinson's Law states that work expands to fill the time available for its completion. This means that if you have one hour to complete a project, you will complete it in one hour. If you are given one day to complete the same project, it will take you one day. And the word "work" can take on several different meanings.

For example, in *Profit First*, Mike Michalowicz uses the analogy of a tube of toothpaste. Got a new tube? The sky's the limit! Load up that toothbrush with all the paste you can fit on it. Getting toward the end? Eh, maybe you don't need to use so much—and you squeeze the life out of the tube hoping to cover maybe a quarter of the brush. The point being that both amounts get the same job done.[6] Sometimes, when I am presenting or speaking on Profit First, I use the analogy of select-a-size paper towels. There's a reason why they cut those sheets in thirds! Brilliant!

Yet another interpretation of this law can be used when referring to the money management approach called "bank balance accounting."

BANK BALANCE ACCOUNTING

Remember earlier, when I mentioned that GAAP makes perfect sense for logical beings who have logical businesses and no cash flow issues? And how that perfectly describes not one restaurateur I know? Instead of GAAP, we restaurateurs have come up with our own way of accounting over time. I call it "bank balance accounting."

How does it work? Well, you log in to your bank accounts on (most likely) a daily basis. When there's money in the account, you spend it. When there isn't, you panic. Sound familiar? This "new" method of accounting is not unique to the restaurant industry. I see it happening in just about every small business I have worked with. But in my experience, the restaurant industry has cornered the market on bank balance accounting. It has become restaurateurs' go-to strategy for cash management.

Here's the problem with this. When you log in to your bank and see your one or two account balances—let's say a total of $10,000, for easy numbers—you automatically think, "Great! I have $10,000 to use. I can make payroll, pay the rent, pay this vendor and that one, maybe order some new glassware." Before you know it, you've spent it all. And by "spent it all," I mean you spent your profit. Because you're not necessarily thinking about profit at this point. Profit may be something you only think about when you look at your P&L. Or maybe you only think about it at the end of the year, for tax reasons.

You might also be spending your own pay and the money you need for taxes, because again, you may not be thinking of those things when you make decisions about what to spend money on. You are simply logging in to your business bank accounts, viewing the available balances, and spending what's there.

Do you see where I'm going with this? Participating in bank balance accounting keeps you in the vicious cycle of constantly chasing that Saturday night because you need those sales to be able to pay the expenses you keep incurring, and you keep incurring those expenses because you keep using up whatever you see in your bank accounts. (That was long-winded, I know; I did that for effect.)

To phrase this differently, when you participate in bank balance accounting, you perpetuate the cycle of just making sales and paying expenses over and over, like a dog chasing its tail. While you may hope that your expenses will be less than your sales, hope doesn't always get you where you want to go, especially with money.

However, you are probably entrenched in this daily or weekly practice of bank balance accounting. It's what you know; it's part of our collective restaurateur DNA by now, and I am not here to break a deeply entrenched habit. No, sir. That's one battle I will stay away from. Instead of trying to break the habit, let's leverage it.

What do I mean by "leverage" it? Well, let's continue to use the bank balance accounting method—but let's also create separate accounts to be used for your restaurant's needs. Let's put intention behind your money. In other words, we will divvy up the money that comes in from sales based on how the money should be used.

Before we get into the nitty-gritty of this life-changing cash management system, though, let's be clear on why *you need to take your profit first.*

WHAT IS PROFIT?

OKAY, OKAY, SO THIS IS the part where I hear a lot of, "But Kasey, if I move money into a separate account and call it profit or something else, I won't have enough left to pay my bills."

Do me a favor and read that again.

This objection tells me that the objector's restaurant is not profitable. And if that's the case, can I ask you something? Why bother? No, really, what's the point? Why have a business that exists solely to pay its expenses? Sounds great if you're a vendor to this place, but for the owner, this business sounds like the proverbial ball and chain.

All businesses need profit to survive, let alone grow.

Here are a few more things you may not know about profit:

- Profit is not greed.
- Profit is required in order to run any business.
- Profit is the only way to service debt. This is not my opinion; it is a fact. If you have any debt, loans, lines of credit, investors, etc., they will not get paid unless you have profit. Want to know the other way to service debt? With more debt.
- Profit is used for capital expenditures such as new (or used) equipment, furniture, computers, leasehold improvements, etc. It is your profit that enables you to afford these things. Without profit, you buy these assets with debt. And how do you pay down debt? Yup, with profit.
- Profit is used to reward your team. Whether you plan for a special activity, a team trip, or a profit-sharing plan that

you use to reward and incentivize your leadership team, profit is *required*. I know firsthand that many business owners wonder about the best way to incentivize their managers and leadership. Profit-sharing is a win-win way to do this.

• Profit is used to reward the owners. I probably should have started with this point, but I feared that if I did, you'd stop reading. Why? Because so many restaurant owners have been slaves to their restaurants for so long that the thought of getting paid regularly, let alone taking a profit distribution, is foreign to them. It shouldn't be. And continuing along this path is 100% counterproductive to creating a restaurant that thrives.

I understand that what I am throwing at you is probably something completely new and different from how you currently think about the money in your restaurant. And given that you are most likely stretching every dollar as far as it can go, managing your money differently might seem daunting. I would argue, though, that you've done much harder things. You've faced tougher challenges. And yet here you are, reading this book, searching for a better way. You found it. And here's how I know you can do it.

A TYPICAL BUSY NIGHT: EVERYTHING GOES WRONG

So, you've got a big night coming up, reservations are sold out, the menu has been created, and all eyes are on this big night ahead. And this will not be just any busy night; this is the night when you can potentially make enough money to get caught up on all your vendor bills, easily make payroll, get that oven fixed, and maybe, just maybe, have enough money left over to pay yourself *something*. After all, it's Valentine's Day.

But as luck would have it, one of your cooks called in sick, the dishwasher isn't working, the health inspector showed up for a "surprise" inspection, your new host no-called/no-showed, the internet is down, and your produce delivery was late, which threw off the entire prep schedule.

Do you shut down and call it a day? Hope that tomorrow will be better? No! Even with all this adversity being thrown at you, you still make it work and the outcome is pretty much the same: a very busy, high-energy night that delivered on your promise to your guests and yielded the same results you projected from the outset.

You can find this scenario in all businesses; shit happens, and you figure out a way to make it work. From my experience, both as a restaurateur and as a consultant for many industries, restaurants tend to "make it work" more often, and in more ways, than your average business. You wrote the book on making it work. You do it all the time, and you do it better than most.

So, if you can perform a sold-out night with limited staff and other unexpected disasters, then you can absolutely manage your money a little differently.

As a matter of fact, by taking your profit first and being forced to operate with the "leftovers," you automatically create the necessary efficiencies to run the restaurant better. These efficiencies not only create the consistency and trust that are key to any restaurant's success (or any business's success, for that matter), they are also where real growth and profitability live.

Let's go get some profit.

CHAPTER 3

This Is the Core Cash Management System that Can Save Your Business

TRADITIONAL BANK BALANCE ACCOUNTING GENERALLY assumes that you have one, maybe two bank accounts. Most restaurants either go all in on one big account where all sales are deposited, and from which all bills, taxes, and payroll are debited, or they have two accounts with that second one just for payroll. I think of this one main operating account as something like a giant platter at your Thanksgiving dinner table. It's got the turkey in the center, a mound of mashed potatoes on one side and a mound of stuffing on the other, maybe some green beans or brussels sprouts, rolls, cranberry sauce, you name it, it's just all piled up on one giant platter. This is your one main restaurant operating account. It contains all your sales (income) and all your expenses.

If you're hungry right now, and if you're a fan of Thanksgiving dinner like my family is, I think you can visualize what I'm putting out there. When it's time to eat, what do you do? Remember, you're starving. If you're like my family, or most people on Thanksgiving, you grab a plate and start piling it with all that deliciousness from your platter. And then you remember that you have guests, so you start filling their plates until the giant platter is empty. Talk about fat and happy. Now everyone is satiated.

But wait, you forgot that Uncle Jim and Aunt Heather are arriving late and need to be fed. You also promised your elderly neighbor that you'd drop by with some leftovers, and you had planned on making turkey sandwiches tomorrow for your book club meeting—but there's nothing left! You and the few people who were lucky enough to be at the table when you set down the platter were the only ones who got to eat (and you are stuffed).

What if, instead of putting all your eggs in one basket, or all your turkey and fixings on one plate, you began by setting aside a couple of plates for Uncle Jim and Aunt Heather? And for your neighbors? And what if you also set aside just enough turkey and stuffing to make those sandwiches for your book club? *Then* you could pile the remaining turkey, stuffing, mashed potatoes, vegetables, rolls, cranberry sauce, etc. on your big platter, set that down in the middle of the table, and enjoy Thanksgiving with your guests. Would that work? Of course it would. The worst thing that could happen is, you and your guests might be just a tad less stuffed but still perfectly content. You might even have room for dessert! And your relatives, neighbors, and book club attendees would all get to enjoy a little Thanksgiving with you and because of you—win, win, win.

This tactic goes back to Parkinson's Law, which I mentioned in the last chapter. For the purposes of this book, another way to interpret this law is "we consume what we see."

With this law in mind, understanding our predilection for bank balance accounting, *and* factoring in the use of only one or two bank accounts for all the expenses it takes to run a restaurant, can you see where the cannibalization takes place? You work your asses off on a Saturday night (or busy week or weekend) to fill up that one bank account (the Thanksgiving platter) only to consume every last morsel by paying every expense, which leaves you with an empty platter (bank account). And now you have to do it all over again! Work your butt off, fill the bank account, spend the money, repeat.

And while you may (hopefully) review your P&L, balance sheet, and cash flow statements every month or so and promise to do better next month, the damage is already done. *We can fix this right now.*

Instead of having only one or two bank accounts, the traditional Profit First system calls for five bank accounts at your current or local bank, plus three remote savings accounts at a hard-to-get-to or online bank. Consider each one of these accounts a "small plate" that will help you divvy up the money that comes into your restaurant and earmark it for specific purposes.

If you just gasped at the number of bank accounts I mentioned above, well, you wouldn't be the first. Let me set your mind at ease.

This system is most likely new to you and anything new, especially when it comes to money, can be a tad frightening. I get that, and I encounter some trepidation in almost every client I work with —at first. But I can tell you from not only firsthand experience, but also my experience working with hundreds of businesses who have implemented this system: There is nothing to be afraid of. This method works better, way better, than any other cash management system I have come across over the last twenty-five years. It will make everything, including your accounting, your cash flow, and your profitability, easier. That's right. Easier—and more consistent. I understand you might still be hesitant but stay with me. I will show you how it works, not just technically but in examples and client stories throughout this book.

HERE'S HOW THE SYSTEM WORKS

BANK ACCOUNT #1 IS CALLED your "Income Account." This is usually a checking account where all your income is deposited. This is where your credit card processor deposits go, as well as deposits of all your cash and checks from sales. This is the account that piles up the money so you can allocate it appropriately to the other accounts. Any loans, investments, grants, or other deposits that are not considered sales do not belong in this account. (If you do receive funds from loans, investments, grants, etc., I recommend putting these funds in a separate account until you determine the intended use for such funds.)

Bank account #2 is called your "Profit Account." This is usually a checking account. You will transfer a predetermined percentage (explained in Chapter 5) from your Income Account here *first*.

Bank account #3 is called your "Owner's Pay Account." This is a checking account because you will pay yourself, the owner, from this account. Using a predetermined percentage (again, I'll explain this in Chapter 5), you will transfer that amount from your Income Account to this account.

Bank account #4 is called your "Owner's Tax Account." This can either be a checking or savings account. You will transfer a predetermined percentage from your Income Account to this account to pay for the owner's personal tax liabilities.

Bank account #5 is called your "OPEX Account" (for operating expenses). The balance left in your Income Account after your transfers to the Profit Account, the Owner's Pay Account, and the Owner's Tax Account will be transferred to this account to pay all the restaurant's expenses. This is your new Thanksgiving platter, and you can gorge yourself on it since we took care of the important stuff *first*, in bank accounts #2 through #4.

After you set up these accounts at your local bank, you will see five accounts instead of one or two when you log in to your online banking. You'll want to nickname them like this:

1. Income Account
2. Profit Account
3. Owner's Pay Account
4. Owner's Tax Account
5. OPEX Account

Welcome to Bank of Money USA!

		Current Balance:
Account ***123	Income Account	$0.00
Account ***456	Profit Account	$0.00
Account ***567	Owners Pay Account	$0.00
Account ***678	Owners Tax Account	$0.00
Account ***789	OPEX Account	$0.00

ORDER MATTERS! SERVE SEQUENTIALLY

ONCE YOU HAVE ALL THE above Profit First accounts set up, and all your sales are flowing into your "Income" Account and only that account, you're ready to get started.

The first allocation (transfer) that you will make is to the Profit Account. This is a nonnegotiable, absolute must. And it may be your smallest allocation—1% of whatever is in your Income Account, for example. That doesn't matter. What does matter is that you take your profit first before feeding the other accounts.

Why? Because we need to undo the centuries' worth of "Sales – Expenses = Profit" damage that has been done to small businesses. This damage may even be relevant to large businesses, but I am going to stay in my lane. As I explained in Chapter 2, profit is essential to the success of any business and needs to come first, before expenses. This way, the expenses don't become bloated and devour the profit. Taking your profit first forces your business to run on what's left, and you know what happens when you have less to work with? You automatically look for savings and ways to create efficiencies in your business because you must. And you know what happens when you create a lean, efficient business? You create a very strong, healthy, profitable business.

The second allocation will be to your Owner's Pay Account. Why? Because the owner birthed this business and continues to breathe life into it and put everything they have into it. They need to be compensated accordingly. And if this allocation isn't made, the owner gets the leftovers—which is usually nothing, or less than nothing (debt). Another reason to ensure that the owner is paid first and foremost (after profit) is so they can become the best version of themselves, and bring that version to work and leadership every day. Not having to carry the weight of worry and stress of not being able to pay the restaurant's bills—and, by extension, not being able to pay themselves—frees up the owner to focus on the bigger picture and bring their vision of hospitality to life on every shift. Only the best version of themselves will create the best version of their business.

The other side of that coin rings true as well. I am sad to say that in my many years of restaurant management and ownership, it is this other side that I have witnessed the most: the owners who give everything they've got to open their restaurants—blood, sweat, tears, money, debt—and don't take any pay until there's "enough money." And, as I explained earlier, there is almost never enough money to do so because their expenses consume all the income. (This is what has created the never-ending search for another Saturday night, which is still never enough.)

Working constantly for no pay begins to breed resentment in restaurant owners, and can we blame them? They've literally given everything to their restaurants and rarely get any return on their blood, sweat, and tears investment. That would create bitterness in anyone. And while this resentment may or may not be conscious, it's still very much there and very harmful to the business.

This isn't to say that the owners should live like kings and queens, though kudos to you if that becomes the case. The owner's pay allocation, *and we will determine the proper percentage for your restaurant in Chapter 5,* needs to be appropriate based on the business model and other factors that we will dive into in later chapters. The last point I want to make about this allocation is, if you ever wish to sell your restaurant or look for investors, one of the main items buyers, banks, and investors look at is the amount that owners pay themselves. The number needs to be fair, consistent, and attractive to a potential buyer or investor.

The third allocation will be to your Owner's Tax Account. This is *not* for your meals tax or sales tax and certainly not for your business's payroll taxes. This account is to be used for the owner's tax liabilities that are incurred from their pay and profit. Now, this isn't to say that you get to "write off" or "expense" your taxes. You don't. But that doesn't mean that your business shouldn't pay for them. Those are two different things. People often get confused on this point. To say it in another way, your business should take care of paying your taxes, and it can if you manage the cash properly. You won't see these tax payments as expenses on your P&L, however. They will be posted on your books as owner's draws or distributions.

The fourth allocation of the Profit First Cash Management System at your local bank is to your OPEX Account. This final allocation should bring your Income Account balance to zero, while the other four accounts—Profit, Owner's Pay, Owner's Tax, and OPEX—will all have balances.

The OPEX Account is used to pay the business's expenses. Just one of the many incredible effects of this system is that if you find there isn't enough money being allocated to your OPEX Account to pay all the bills, you'll know that you've got a problem right away. It is *so* much better to know this sooner than later. In fact, it's imperative to be aware of this problem immediately rather than discover it when the month is closed. Without the Profit First allocations and depending on when your bookkeeper can reconcile the accounts, you could be halfway through the next month before you notice a problem that could have been addressed earlier.

Another benefit of using this system is, when you find there isn't enough money in the OPEX Account to cover the bills, you must make a decision—an important one. Which account will you take money from to cover the shortfall? Will it be your Profit Account? Because as it stands now, your profit is most likely where any make-up funds are coming from, and without you even realizing it. Or will you take it out of your Owner's Pay Account? Or maybe you prefer to take it out of your Owner's Tax Account, knowing that you could be in trouble come tax time?

Another benefit of this system is that it causes you to prioritize spending time on analyzing your expenses, trimming and cutting wherever possible so that the next time you allocate, you won't have to "borrow" from another account. This exercise in reviewing expenses, cutting what you don't really need, looking for efficiencies, and streamlining wherever you can reaps so many other benefits. Not only does it save you money, which makes your business leaner, meaner (as they say), and more profitable, it also gets your brain thinking in a different way than it probably has in a while.

This new way of thinking—looking ahead, looking for improvements, looking to be more innovative—is a far cry from the "Let's just keep from drowning until Saturday gets here" mentality. This mindset shift alone can change everything. Instead of being in a constant state of struggle, treading water until the next wave of cash flows in and always having that pit of anxiety, despair, and worry in your stomach, you'll feel a sense of security and be more focused on the positive aspects of your business.

Streamlining and cutting costs is like trimming the fat. It leaves you lighter, stronger, and more agile. Creating innovation anywhere in your business is always a great thing. Plus, while all this internal work may seem like it's just that—internal tweaks and fixes that are invisible to your customers—the outcome is most certainly visible and creates the most positive effects.

Here is a myth I'd like to bust: Cutting and/or streamlining expenses does *not* equate to providing an inferior customer experience. Not at all. As a matter of fact, streamlining your business can often enhance it.

Here's an example. Let's say your paper goods line item seems high when you review your expenses. When you drill into the detail on your expense reports you notice that the super-duper, triple-ply, trifold bathroom towels are quite expensive and you're going through a *lot* of them. Now, you've been so busy worrying about everything, rather than taking the time to zero in on the small stuff that can have a big impact, that you are shocked to realize it would be cheaper for you to buy a similar paper towel, maybe two-ply, maybe just bifold, *with your logo on it*. Switching to the new towel could save you up to 25% on your paper goods line item, *and* you'll have towels with your logo on them! You'll also be that much closer to having enough money in your OPEX Account on allocation day to cover all your expenses rather than having to "borrow" from your other accounts. (By the way, consider the quotation marks around "borrow" air quotes. You and I both know the chances of you paying that money back are nil.)

Here is a sample screenshot of your bank accounts *prior to* your initial allocations:

Income Account	$10,000.00
Profit Account	$0.00
Owners Pay Account	$0.00
Owners Tax Account	$0.00
OPEX Account	$2,056.98

Here is a sample screenshot of your bank accounts *after* your initial allocations:

Income Account	$0.00	
Profit Account	$1,000.00	(assuming 10% profit)
Owners Pay Account	$3,000.00	(assuming 30% owner's pay)
Owners Tax Account	$1,000.00	(assuming 10% owner's tax)
OPEX Account	$7,056.98	(assuming 50% OPEX)

REMOVE TEMPTATION

Okay, so now that we've covered your primary, local bank accounts and allocations, there are two more transfers you will want to make on a weekly or biweekly basis. These are to the "out of sight, out of mind" savings accounts.

Here's how they work. At a separate, "remote" bank, open three high interest-bearing savings accounts. Nickname these accounts as follows:

1. Profit Savings Account
2. Tax Savings Account
3. Reserve Funds Savings Account (or Vault Account)

A remote bank is one such as American Express, Discover, Synchrony Bank, etc. These are mainly non-brick-and-mortar banks that offer online products such as this type of savings account. And because they are not traditional brick-and-mortar banks, which have higher overhead, they are able to offer better products such as the no-minimum balance, no-fee, high interest-bearing accounts. (Don't get too excited, the interest you earn won't be huge, but it will certainly be better than nothing.)

The main reason I recommend these types of accounts is to keep your money safely "locked" away from you. Well, for a few days, anyway. When you make transfers to these accounts, it takes a couple of business days to process them between your local bank and your remote savings bank. And the same is true when you initiate a return transfer. We highly recommend these types of accounts for exactly this reason. We don't want you to have the ability to have instantaneous access to these funds as all kinds of crazy emotional things can happen. By removing the quick access to your profit and your taxes, we are safeguarding them.

After you complete your initial transfers using your local bank accounts, you will then log in to your remote savings bank and initiate two transfers. The first transfer will be from your local-bank Profit Account to your remote Profit Savings Account. The second transfer will be from your local Owner's Tax Account to your remote Tax Savings Account.

These funds will accumulate in these accounts for an entire quarter. Here's what happens at the end of each quarter:

1. If you have debt in your business, you will transfer about 95% of the profit that has accumulated in your remote Profit Savings Account to your local Profit Account. You will use this 95% to pay off your high-interest debt first. The remaining 5% can be used in one of two ways.

   The first is to transfer it to your new, remote Reserve Funds Savings Account and leave it there. Reserve funds are your "rainy day" or emergency funds that every business should have for just those reasons: rain or snow days (with unexpected, slower sales or weather damage) and emergencies. This account is also a great way to create your own line of credit for your restaurant instead of borrowing via a line of credit from your bank.

   The second is to transfer the remaining 5% to your local Profit Account and use it to reward yourself, your team, or however you choose. After all, as I said earlier, profit serves so many purposes in a business. Two of those are servicing debt and rewarding the owner and/or the team.

2. If there is no debt in the business, first, congratulations. You are in the minority, and I love it. Here is how we utilize

the profit: Transfer 50% to your Reserve Funds Savings Account; then transfer the other 50% to your local Profit Account, where you may do with it as you please. Share it, don't share it, throw a party or go on vacation—you have earned this money by owning and running a kick-ass business, so the choice is up to you. But whatever you do, try not to put it back into the business. That would be counter to this entire process, and there are other ways to invest in your business besides continually putting the profit back in. It's time to stop and smell the roses! You'll be a better operator if you do.

3. Okay, so now for the taxes. If you are familiar with making estimated quarterly tax payments to the federal and state (if applicable) governments, then you already know what to do. At the end of the quarter, transfer all the funds from your remote Tax Savings Account back to your local Owner's Tax Account and then make your estimated tax payments using these funds. Easy-breezy. If you are unfamiliar with the process of making quarterly estimated tax payments, we will go over that in Chapter 11.

IT'S ALL ABOUT RHYTHM

By now, you've learned what the Profit First Cash Management System is and what accounts you need to set up so you can run the system. Now the question is, when do you run it? When do you make these allocations/transfers? Daily? Weekly? Monthly? Whenever you feel like it? As with any good system, there needs to be a method to your madness. (Profit First is not madness, that just sounded good.)

What we want to do is establish a rhythm. We want to set guidelines for when these important allocations will be made. The best way to do this, according to *Profit First*, is to make your allocations on the 10th and 25th of each month. The reasoning behind these dates is that they are spread out equally, and most bills are due either at mid-month (around the 15th) or on the first of the month. Allocating the funds on the 10th and 25th allows enough time for the money to enter your OPEX Account so you can send payments to your vendors on time.[7]

This system is cash flow at its most visually fluid. When you perform your allocations according to an established routine, you can see the cash move through your business via the bank accounts. As a result, you will gain a new understanding of, and dare I say appreciation for, how you treat this income. Many believe that cash flow is the lifeblood of any business. As a small business bookkeeper, accountant, and consultant for over fifteen years, I can tell you that this is absolutely true.

There is a very successful personal budgeting app called YNAB ("You Need a Budget"). The way this app was designed is actually kinda genius, and it has some similarities to Profit First. You can look it up and learn about it yourself if you're interested. I mention this because I once heard the founder of YNAB speak and something he said really resonated with me. He talked about giving every dollar a job. And that is exactly what we are doing here. We are giving a very specific job to every dollar that comes into your restaurant.

As is often true, when you put intention behind something, transformation happens. So when we put intention behind your dollar and call it profit, well, we create a profitable business. My guess is that, before you started reading this book—and without realizing it—the intention you were putting behind every dollar was payment for expenses.

THE FIVE FOUNDATIONAL ACCOUNTS (+3)

WE HAVE COVERED A LOT in this chapter—the main architecture of the core Profit First System. Let's review.

The five foundational accounts (at your local bank) are:

1. Income Account (checking or savings)
2. Profit Account (checking or savings)
3. Owner's Pay Account (checking)
4. Owner's Tax Account (checking or savings)
5. OPEX Account (checking)

Each of these accounts should be free, no-fee, no-minimum balance bank accounts. If your current bank does not offer free checking or savings accounts, there are plenty of banks that do. You can find the list of Profit First-friendly banks I curated for you on my website at www.profitfirst4restaurants.com (click on "Tools").

Then there are the three out of sight, out of mind remote savings accounts. Each of these accounts should be free, no-fee, no-minimum balance accounts that pay the highest interest rate you can find:

1. Profit Savings Account
2. Owner's Tax Savings Account
3. Reserve Funds (or Vault) Savings Account

It is helpful to nickname these accounts on your banking log-in screen *and* use the same nicknames when adding the accounts to your accounting software, such as QuickBooks. This makes it that much easier for you, your bookkeeper, or your accountant to record the transfers between accounts.

Not sure where to find accounts like the ones referenced above? No worries! Not only did my team create a list of Profit First-friendly banks across the United States; we also created a "Profit First Banking Setup Checklist" to make setting up your accounts easy-breezy. Go to www.profitfirst4restaurants.com and click on "Tools" to download yours.

FREAKED OUT YET?

STILL THINKING THIS IS TOO much? Feeling overwhelmed, or like your bookkeeper or accountant might kill you if you open all these accounts? Are you worried that your banker will look at you like you have three heads or are attempting to do something shady when you go in to open your accounts? These are some of the initial objections I have heard over the years, but neither of the aforementioned scenarios have ever come true. Well, hold on a second. A few old-school bookkeepers or accountants out there may still believe in green ledger paper and one bank account. And with great respect, I submit to you that they are 100% wrong. These are the same people who believe that GAAP accounting makes perfect sense. And they are correct in that GAAP makes perfect logical, mathematical sense in a world where nothing goes wrong and cash flow is as smooth and free-flowing as the Nile. If you're reading this book, you know that is not the reality of the restaurant business.

The thing is, by now, many bookkeepers, accountants, and even banks have heard of Profit First. It is that well-known *because it works,* and people are talking about it and recommending it all over the world, not just in the US. When you go to your local branch to open your accounts, bring a copy of this book with you, or maybe even just the download of the Profit First Banking Setup Checklist, if you feel you need to. This single page of instructions should give your banker enough information to understand the Profit First concept and what you are looking to achieve. In addition, many banks are "graded" or "bonused" by their district or regional bosses based on the number of accounts they open in any given period, so instead of the stink eye, you might get a giant bear hug.

If I have not yet convinced you that this system will change everything for you and your business, can you do just one thing for me? Well, for you, really. Just open one additional account and nickname it "Profit." It is preferable to use one of the remote savings accounts, but any account will work. Then transfer just 1% of whatever you have in your current account over to your Profit Account. When more money comes in, see if you can transfer just 1% of those deposits to this account as well. And please email me at kasey@profitfirst4restaurants.com to let me know this is done. I will check in on you periodically to see how this is going and cheer you on to greater profits!

If you're ready to jump in headfirst but feel like you might need your hand held here and there along the way, join our monthly MacDaddy Office Hours membership. My team and I set aside a few hours every month with one of our Master-certified Profit First Professional accountants, who is there to answer all your questions and support you as you build profitability in your restaurant. You can join the monthly MacDaddy Office Hours membership by going to www.profitfirst4restaurants.com and clicking on "Shop."

Still with me and ready to make some money? Good. Let's blow this up.

PROFIT FIRST SUCCESS STORY

Bar NYC

A COUPLE OF YEARS AGO, the owners of a large sports bar and restaurant located in New York City came to us for help. They had read *Profit First*, and while a bit skeptical about whether it might work for them, they decided to give it a try. As with all the businesses and restaurants we work with, we first must get hold of the numbers via not only cleaning up and organizing the bookkeeping, but also by completing a Profit Assessment (you will learn about this in Chapter 5). A Profit (or Instant) Assessment is a broad yet simple way to view where the money has gone in your business.

As is quite common, the owners of Bar NYC were surprised to see that their prime costs (food, beverage, and labor) were higher than they had thought, and that their overall profit was quite low, almost nonexistent. Were there a few months where they made a profit? Sure. But they ran at a loss during just as many months, and when we looked at the whole year, the losses won out.

Once their Profit Assessment was done and we knew where they were bleeding money, they were able to act. Their food cost was a little high, so they worked with the kitchen manager and cooks to go over all the menu items.

They adjusted prices, ingredients, and portion sizes, and then they were on their way to a better food cost within days.

Their payroll was also quite high. The non-operating owner, who was more of an investor, was taking a large salary that the restaurant simply could not afford. Through implementing Profit First, we knew what the restaurant *could* afford to pay its owners each week. Kitchen labor was also on the high side, and while they didn't want to lose staff, they figured out a way to schedule better. By shortening some kitchen shifts, they were able to save a few percentage points on their payroll cost.

Our client also completed an expense analysis (you will learn about this in Chapter 9) and definitely found some potential ways to save, but the bigger benefit was the exercise of going through each line item. The act of focusing on which expenses were important to keep and which could be let go was illuminating. Plus, moving forward, the owners were much more likely to scrutinize every new expense and make the most of their existing expenses, which we knew would help keep the restaurant nimble, lean, and in fighting shape.

The results? About nine months in to implementing Profit First, this restaurant was running more smoothly than it had ever before. Cash was flowing much more easily. New focus and controls helped to create a less frantic and panicked atmosphere, which brought the general stress level down. Now the work was more enjoyable—dare I say, relaxing—for the staff, which translated into more caring and love showing up in the food, the drinks, the clean tables, the happy hosts, you name it. As this joyful, calm demeanor trickled down to the guests, sales increased while expenses decreased. The difference was profit.

When the owners of this restaurant first came to us, they had $5,570 in their bank account and almost $100,000 in payables owed to vendors, and they were running at a $50,000 annual loss. One year after implementing Profit First, they had $184,000 in their bank accounts, payables of only $27,659, and an annual profit of $96,551.

Bar NYC	Before PF	After PF
Bank Balance	$5,570	$184,000
Accounts Payable	$100,000+	$27,659
Net Income/Profit	($50,000)	$96,551

CHAPTER 4

This Is the Cash Management System on Restaurant Steroids

INTRODUCING MACDADDY PF CASH

Now that you understand the concept and core of Profit First, let's take it up a notch or two. While I adore the core Profit First system and used that to get myself started years ago, as soon as you see its benefits—and you will early on—you will start to see ways to leverage it even more.

For restaurants, that can mean several things, i.e., opening several more accounts. You don't have to do this right away. You can absolutely get started with the core system and be happy there. The most important thing is to just get started. But if you're an overachiever like me, a "go big or go home"-type person, or if you've already been doing the core and want something more (hey, that rhymed)—in other words, if you are the "MacDaddy"—then here's what I have for you.

MEALS TAX ACCOUNT

First, there is the meals tax. I have yet to meet a state that does not impose some type of tax on restaurant meals or beverages. This is a tax, money, that you collect from your customers and then hand over to the state, town, county, or however it works where your restaurant is located. While it may not always feel like it, this money was never yours to begin with. You are simply acting as a trustee of this money for the government, and not playing by their rules is nothing short of extremely harmful to you and your restaurant. Let's not go there.

Instead, open a checking account and call it "Meals Tax Account" or "Sales Tax Account" (whatever term you use to identify these taxes should also be used as the nickname for the account). These taxes are a percentage of your customers' checks, your sales, and therefore it should be easy to assign an allocation percentage to the account. For example, here in Massachusetts we have a state meals tax of 6.25%. Many towns then adopted a "local" meals tax of .75% to make it an even 7.0% meals tax. Again, because this is not your money and we don't want to fool around with it, this will be the first allocation you make, right off the top.

PRIME COST: PAYROLL ACCOUNT

PAYROLL IS A MAJOR FACTOR in many businesses and especially the restaurant business. Like the meals tax, which is "not your money" either, setting aside payroll expenses right away is a great habit to master.

Your schedule should be designed so you have less labor on slower nights and more on busier nights. That way, the percentage you allocate for payroll will stay in line with your financial model. This could mean that on some nights you run at 40% labor and 25% on others, but across the payroll period (weekly or biweekly) it averages about 30% in most restaurants. If you are operating your restaurant accordingly, then you should have a good idea of your payroll percentage.

Your Payroll Account percentage should include every element of the payroll sweep—i.e., salaries and wages, including management (but not owner's pay); payroll taxes; fees; 401(k) matches; and whatever else comes from your total payroll debit. If you're heading into a slower season, maybe you bump the allocation up to 32% just to make sure you're covered in your Payroll Account. Again, I am just using these percentages as examples. Maybe your payroll percentage is higher or lower. You will figure this out when you do your Instant Assessment in the next chapter.

And here is another thing I love about this system. Let's say you run a 30% payroll all-in. Therefore, you allocate thirty cents on every dollar to your Payroll Account from the Income Account (after allocating to your Meals Tax Account). And then let's say you run your payroll and realize that the total payroll requirements are more than the 30% you just transferred into your Payroll Account. What do you do?

Obviously, you can't short the payroll, so you need to transfer more money into the Payroll Account to cover it. But where will you take the money from? Your OPEX Account? Maybe. But then you'll have less to pay your vendors. Your Owner's Pay Account? That won't feel very good. Your Owner's Tax Account? That's never a good idea, but my guess is that might be the one you'll go for; personal taxes can sometimes seem like an illusion since they don't require payment as frequently as regular vendors or payroll. Or will you take it from your Profit Account? Without using this system, that's exactly where payroll funding comes from—out of profit. You'll see that your payroll percentage is too high, and your net profit is too low, when you review your P&L. Of course, you won't see this until your books are closed for the period and you have time to review the financials which can be, what, maybe a few weeks or even a month or two later?

When you use MacDaddy PF Cash, you know *instantly* that payroll is too high and can take action to fix it right away, before a few more weeks or months go by and you realize what's happening. Just imagine all the money, stress, and issues you can save yourself and your restaurant by having this crucial information right away and literally at your fingertips!

PRIME COST: COGS (FOOD AND BEVERAGE) ACCOUNT

I LOVE THE COGS (COST of goods sold) Account. It acts as a living, breathing budget for your food and beverage costs. Much like the Payroll Account described above, you assign your food and beverage cost percentage to this account. If you believe (and/or if your financial history tells you) that you run a 30% combined food and beverage cost, then you simply transfer thirty cents on every dollar to this account. You then use this account to pay your food and beverage vendors.

Not enough money in your COGS Account to cover what you owe your food and beverage vendors? Then guess what? You're not running a 30% combined food and beverage cost. And wouldn't you rather know this piece of extremely important information *now* rather than wait to view it on a P&L or income statement that you may or may not look at weeks or months from now?

If you realize, after one or two weeks of allocating the 30%, that you don't have enough to cover what is owed, you can and should make some strategic decisions to right this wrong. Here are just some of the things you can do to turn this around quickly:

- Do a deep dive into all your vendor invoices to make sure that you are being charged the prices they quoted you.
- Review the invoices and credit slips to ensure that you are receiving all the proper credits.
- Run a menu mix to review which items were sold the most over that period and run the individual food or beverage cost on those items to see if they are too high.
- Complete a proper, full, physical inventory to see if you purchased too much of something and either return it or run a special.
- Create and run food or drink specials that have a higher profit margin to immediately counteract the overall high costs you are incurring while simultaneously reviewing and costing every item on your menu to get its true item cost. (It may be time to revamp your menus or adjust the pricing.)

I could go on and on with adding accounts to give you "live" budgets, but I don't want to overwhelm you and believe me, I do know how overwhelming this might feel to you right now. *Stay with me.*

If you are like many restaurateurs, it's practically a daily task to keep the one or two bank accounts you currently do have from incurring overdraft fees. You are not going to have any less money, it's all still there, you are just going to manage it differently. And when you separate out your money based on your intention for it, i.e., food and beverage costs, payroll, operating expenses, etc., you will get so much more clarity on your financials. This will allow you to act quickly and exactly where action needs to be taken. So start with either the five core Profit First accounts or with MacDaddy PF Cash, and build your financial muscles there first.

Based on the premise that additional accounts can act as living, breathing budgets for you, you can apply this ideology to other areas of your business as well. For example, if you want to ensure that your marketing and advertising costs are in line, or even if you want to know what you *can* spend on marketing and advertising, set an allocation budget amount, maybe 5%, and that account will give you the budget you want to spend on advertising. I also love the idea of creating a "Company Culture Account" or even a "Giving Back/Charity Account" to which you allocate maybe just 1% and let it build over time. This gives you and your team time to decide on the best use for these funds, too. Before you realize it, you may have enough built up to throw a really great employee appreciation party and/or donate to a favorite charity.

Another one of my favorites is a "New Employee Account." If you are in a position where, for example, you feel like you want to hire a manager or another sous chef but aren't sure you can really afford it, then open a New Employee Account. Every time you allocate, you make one additional transfer either from your Payroll or OPEX Account, depending on the position you are seeking to hire for, and transfer what you would pay for this position to that new account. This account now serves two purposes. The first is that it allows you to see if you can currently afford this new position. Second, if you determine that you can afford it, you will have at least a few weeks' worth of funds saved up to pay this person when they come on board and begin training.

These add-on or "advanced" accounts are used for the areas of your business where you *can* control the costs. It's setting an intention and specific purpose for every dollar that comes in. And again, when we set intentions and follow through, that's where change and growth happen.

These accounts would not work as well if you created them for every cost you have, such as rent or insurance, since those are generally fixed rather than percentage-based costs and are considered true operating costs. True operating costs should be paid from your OPEX Account.

Before I mention a few more optional accounts, now is a good time to recap what our new cash management infrastructure may look like.

While the core Profit First Cash Management System looks like this:

Five Foundational (local) bank accounts:

1. Income Account (checking or savings)
2. Profit Account (checking or savings)
3. Owner's Pay Account (checking)
4. Owner's Tax Account (checking or savings)
5. OPEX Account (checking)

And three remote bank savings accounts:

1. Profit Savings Account
2. Tax Savings Account
3. Reserve Funds Savings Account (or Vault Account),

The MacDaddy PF Cash Management System looks like this:

Eight local bank accounts:

1. Income Account (checking or savings)
2. Meals Tax Account (checking or savings)
3. Payroll Account (checking)
4. COGS/Food and Beverage Account (checking)
5. Profit Account (checking or savings)
6. Owner's Pay Account (checking)
7. Owner's Tax Account (checking or savings)
8. OPEX Account (checking)

And three remote bank savings accounts:

1. Profit Savings Account
2. Tax Savings Account
3. Reserve Funds Savings Account (or Vault Account)

Go to www.profitfirst4restaurants.com and click on "Tools" to download your free MacDaddy PF Cash Banking Setup Instructions sheet.

Again, whether you choose the core Profit First system or go for it with MacDaddy PF Cash, that's all you need to do right now: Pick one system, open the accounts, and get started. I know I'm not asking for a little. It's a lot. And if there were some other way— any other way—to get the same results in a quicker, simpler, easier fashion, I'd be writing a different book. I'd probably have billboards up, because who doesn't like a quick, easy fix? I know I do. But this is as close as it gets, and I promise you, it's not as hard as it may seem to you at this moment. And once your accounts are set up and you roll through a couple of allocations, you'll see what I mean. It will make your finances so much clearer and easier.

While this book is your how-to resource on implementing MacDaddy PF Cash in your restaurant and includes everything you need to know to build and run the system, I am aware that there can be speed bumps in the process or unique cases that I may not have addressed. For these reasons, and because I want to support as many restaurateurs as I can, I offer a monthly membership to our MacDaddy Office Hours where you can show up and bring all your questions. My team has the answers. Go to www.profitfirst4restaurants.com and click on "Shop" to sign up.

IF YOU'RE FEELING SUPER SASSY: ADVANCED PROFIT FIRST ACCOUNTS

THERE IS A SAYING IN the Profit First world: "When in doubt, open an account." At this point, I do not recommend that you adopt this adage. You must walk before you can run, and I believe this phrase was coined and popularized by people who were already running Profit First and experienced so much success that they just took it and ran with it. That's all well and great, but when you're just getting started, I believe that slow(ish) and steady wins the race.

That said, I would be remiss if I didn't at least mention a couple of other areas, or accounts, that could be better managed if separated out from the rest.

SEASONAL ("DRIP") ACCOUNT

If you own or are thinking of owning a restaurant that is seasonal, or somewhat seasonal, you may or may not have been wondering how this system can work for you. Well, here is your answer, and it may be simpler than you think.

Let's say you own a restaurant on Nantucket. Historically speaking, you do 80% of your sales in three months. The other 20% of your sales come during six months, and the remaining three months of the year you are closed. Again, this does not have to be exact, just close enough.

For easy numbers, let's say your restaurant grosses $1,000,000 annually; 80% of $1,000,000 is $800,000, which means that during those three summer months, your gross sales are about $266,667 per month. ($800,000 ÷ 3 = $266,667 per month.)

During those three months, after you allocate to your Meals Tax, COGS, and Payroll Accounts and are left with your real revenue, you will add one more allocation and that will be to your Seasonal Account. (Real revenue is the money your restaurant earns after it pays its *direct* meals or sales tax obligations and its prime costs for a given period. On some P&L reports, real revenue is the same as your "Gross Profit" line item.) This Seasonal Account will act as a sort of rainy-day fund for both your slower and your closed months.

Generally, this allocation comes out of your OPEX allocation, as these funds are used to pay the operating expenses of the business during the off-season. If you didn't have this Seasonal Account and simply funded your OPEX Account, then you'd probably have a very robust balance in your OPEX Account during those summer months. And theoretically speaking, if you were fantastic about controlling your expenses and Parkinson's Law didn't apply to you, you could just leave the money in your OPEX Account and it would still be there when winter rolled around.

But now that you know all about Parkinson's Law and how our nature is to consume what we see, you may suspect that it's an all-around better idea to move the money to the account created for its intended purpose and fund your slower months by way of a "Drip" or Seasonal Account.

To figure out what percentage to allocate to the Seasonal Account, let's do some simple math. You will learn about Profit and Instant Assessments in the next chapter, but here is a sneak peek at a completed Instant Assessment to help us with this example:

		ACTUAL $	TAPs %
Income Bucket	TOP LINE REVENUE/GROSS SALES	$ 1,000,000.00	100%
Bucket 1	COGS (FOOD, LIQ, BEV)	$ 300,000.00	30%
Bucket 2	PAYROLL (EXCL. OWNER)	$ 300,000.00	30%
	REAL REVENUE	$ 400,000.00	40%
Bucket 3	PROFIT	$ 40,000.00	10%
Bucket 4	OWNER'S PAY	$ 140,000.00	35%
Bucket 5	OWNER'S TAXES	$ 60,000.00	15%
Bucket 6	OPEX	$ 160,000.00	40%

If your OPEX expenses are $160,000 annually, then they are about $13,333 per month ($160,000 ÷ 12 = $13,333). Now, presumably, there are some expenses that fall under OPEX that are higher during your in-season months than they are during your off-season months. You can figure out what that looks like if you have historical data from prior seasons. Let's say that for your three in-season months, your operating expenses are about $20,000 per month. Therefore, you want to be sure that during those three summer months, there's about $20,000 in your OPEX Account to cover those expenses. Any remainder will go into your Seasonal Account. Here is what your allocations might look like over those three in-season months.

		ACTUAL $	TAPs %
Income Bucket	TOP LINE REVENUE/GROSS SALES	$ 266,667.00	100%
Bucket 1	COGS (FOOD, LIQ, BEV)	$ 80,000.10	30%
Bucket 2	PAYROLL (EXCL. OWNER)	$ 80,000.10	30%
	REAL REVENUE	$ 106,666.80	40%
Bucket 3	PROFIT	$ 10,666.68	10%
Bucket 4	OWNER'S PAY	$ 37,333.38	35%
Bucket 5	OWNER'S TAXES	$ 16,000.02	15%
Bucket 6	OPEX	$ 21,333.36	20%
Bucket 7	DRIP/SEASONAL	$ 21,333.36	20%

If you use these allocations over those three busy months, then you will have over $60,000 in your Seasonal Account to cover your winter operational expenses. This should not only be enough to cover the expenses for the three months you are closed; there should also be enough to help cover any shortages during the six slower months that you are open.

We will dive deep into your operational expense analysis in Chapter 9. However, it is fair to say that your operational expenses should be somewhat lower during your slower months. In addition, if you are following the MacDaddy PF Cash system, your restaurant will be running as efficiently as possible, and therefore the allocation percentages you use for those six slower months may be different from the ones you use during your high season. They don't necessarily have to be different, but changing it up may be easier on your cash flow.

Again, every restaurant is different, and this is not an exact science. You can design an allocation table that works best for *your* restaurant. For example, if your monthly OPEX allocation for those six slower months ends up being closer to about $10,000 per month, then your allocation table might look something like this:

	6 SLOWER MONTHS	ACTUAL $		TAPs %
Income Bucket	TOP LINE REVENUE/GROSS SALES	$	22,222.22	100%
Bucket 1	COGS (FOOD, LIQ, BEV)	$	6,666.67	30%
Bucket 2	PAYROLL (EXCL. OWNER)	$	6,666.67	30%
	REAL REVENUE	$	8,888.89	40%
Bucket 3	PROFIT	$	888.89	10%
Bucket 4	OWNER'S PAY	$	2,666.67	30%
Bucket 5	OWNER'S TAXES	$	888.89	10%
Bucket 6	*OPEX*	$	4,444.44	50%
Bucket 7	DRIP/SEASONAL	$	–	0%

In this example, using the low sales of the slower months, you are only able to allocate about $4,444 to your OPEX even though you know you need $10,000. Therefore, you transfer $5,600 from your Seasonal Account during each slower month to cover your OPEX expenses. $5,600 x 6 months = $33,600. If you do this for the six months that you anticipate will be slower, you'll be left with a balance of about $26,400 ($60,000 – $33,600 = $26,400) in your Seasonal account to cover the three months you are closed. That will give you approximately $8,800 per month ($26,400 ÷ by three months = $8,800) to cover operating expenses during the three months that you are closed.

Let me be clear: This was just one example using easy, round numbers. If you have operated your seasonal restaurant for a while, you have historical data you can use to uncover what amount and what seasonal allocation percentages you will need to meet your needs during your next off-season period.

Gift Cards/Certificates Liability Account

Some restaurants really knock it out of the park with gift card sales. Around the holidays, many restaurants are open and staffed during extra hours just to accommodate the insatiable demand for gift cards. Sometimes this unique spike in sales can feel like pennies from heaven! But here's the thing, calling them "gift card sales" is a misnomer. Because technically, an actual "sale" is not recognized until the gift card is redeemed. What that means is, every time a gift card or gift certificate is sold, it is recorded as a liability on your balance sheet. Another way to look at it is, as soon as a gift card is sold and carried out into the world, it's like a mini debt. You, the restaurant, now owe the holder of that gift card the value, or amount, that the gift card was purchased for. Once that gift card is redeemed, it releases the restaurant of that liability, and now whatever the guest purchased with that gift card becomes income and can be recorded as a sale.

None of this accounting mumbo jumbo has a whole lot of meaning when you're selling a nominal amount of gift cards. You sell a few one month, a few are redeemed the following month, and it all comes out in the wash. However, when you sell $50,000 worth of gift cards in a short period of time, you may need to stop and consider what I mentioned in the above paragraph. You may have sold $50,000, but you now have a $50,000 liability. In this instance, taking the windfall of $50,000 and transferring it to a separate "Gift Card Account" is the safest move. Then, each week, each month, or even daily, if that works for you, you determine the total of the gift cards that have been redeemed and simply move that amount from your Gift Card Account to your Income Account and allocate it along with the rest of your income.

Simply put, if you run a weekly report from your point-of-sale that shows that $1,500 has been redeemed in gift cards for that week, you will transfer $1,500 from your Gift Card Account to your Income Account. If you use a bank that allows for no minimum balances and no fees, you can keep this account open until the next holiday season rolls around or use it to hold deposits on any large parties or events that you book throughout the year. You get the picture.

DELIVERY FEES

AT THE TIME OF THIS writing, deliveries via DoorDash, Grubhub, Uber Eats, and other food delivery services are at an all-time high following the height of the COVID-19 pandemic, and their often-astronomical fees are a hot-button topic both within the industry and at the government level. It's new territory at this point, given that our culture has quickly become accustomed to food delivery on a regular basis, and to meet this new demand, restaurants need to utilize these large, organized delivery services. And with capitalism working at its best, these delivery services are taking full advantage.

This put restaurants in a very tough position. They need the service, and they're going to pay through the nose for it. Hopefully, and I do believe this will happen, independent restaurants and these delivery services will come to some kind of win-win agreement and move forward with prosperity for both. Most likely it will be the end user, the guest, who pays the price both literally and figuratively. But that's a decision for the guest to make. If they want that convenience, they'll decide its value.

I do not recommend opening a separate account for these fees. As of now, these fees are closely tied to the income associated with them. Oftentimes, the delivery service takes their fee before depositing the net sale into your account, so you never actually see it. But just because you don't see it doesn't mean it isn't there. It is. When you enter into an agreement with a delivery service, or with any service for that matter, be sure you fully understand what that means for your restaurant and adjust your financials, your business model, accordingly. You will learn all about your unique business model in Chapter 7, but for now, just be aware that these fees exist and most likely cannot be absorbed, and that you will need to adjust accordingly.

And finally, I would be completely remiss if I did not address the number one pushback of all time…

SPREADSHEETS ARE NOT THE ANSWER

"WHY SO MANY ACCOUNTS? WHY can't we just do this thing using a spreadsheet?"

These are probably the two most common questions or responses I get when teaching or even just talking about Profit First.

I think I've demonstrated why you need so many accounts. The answer to the second question is: absolutely not.

I will tell you why. Using a spreadsheet instead of the accounts defeats the entire purpose of Profit First. A spreadsheet is manipulable, meaning that you can, whether consciously or unconsciously, adjust it to fit your desired outcome. There is no accountability with a spreadsheet—not like there is when you're using real money in real bank accounts. And most importantly, using multiple bank accounts leverages the habit you already have, the one ingrained in your DNA since you became a business owner: logging in to your bank account, looking at the balance, and making questionable decisions based on the amount you see.

This system is all about intention and purpose. It's basically the equivalent of putting your money where your mouth is.

These bank accounts act as your working, live budgets. Once you log in to your bank and make your allocations, a task that will take you less than five or ten minutes, intention and purpose are placed behind every dollar. You'll know if you hit your food and labor cost targets because there will be enough money in those accounts to cover what you owe for those expenses. If there isn't enough money to cover them, you have to make a very real decision about where you'll pull the money from so you can pay those vendors and your employees. That means that your other bank account balances will go down so that these can go up. Making these kinds of adjustments shows you, in real time, what your business can afford and what it cannot. Can you make these adjustments in a spreadsheet? Sure you can. But where is the lesson in that? How do you really *feel* it and fully comprehend what your business is telling you when you're simply adjusting figures in a column? And more importantly, your spreadsheet won't overdraw your accounts. (I am certainly not suggesting that you want to overdraw any account, but that is where reality sinks in.) Red ink on a spreadsheet isn't quite the same as looking at your money live on your banking screen and making real-time decisions. The fact is that you won't allow your accounts to be overdrawn if you can help it, so you will be forced to make those tough, necessary decisions and adjust accordingly.

But if you're using just one or two bank accounts—a big "platter" for everything, or maybe one big platter for all your expenses plus a second just for payroll, in tandem with a spreadsheet—to lend intention to your money, you're missing the whole point.

A spreadsheet is theory-based.

Bank accounts are reality-based.

MacDaddy PF Cash is about getting real with your money and your business, getting your head out of the sand, and creating a profitable restaurant.

This is how it's done. Not in theory, but in reality. If you're reading this, it's because you're looking for a better way. And you've found it.

If you want to see real change, real improvements in your restaurant; if you want to see the difference you can make and a clear path forward; if you picked up this book because you thought it might help your restaurant run better, perform better, make more money, and bring the joy back to hospitality, you're on the right track.

Let's keep going.

A Small Restaurant Group with Multiple Owner-Investors

I CONNECTED WITH ANOTHER PROFIT First coach, Ellen Minteer of Off Your Plate Accounting in California, who also specializes in working with restaurants. Ellen was kind enough to share one of her favorite Profit First success stories with me. Here it is.

"I work with a small restaurant group that grosses about $6 million in annual sales among three restaurants. Two of the restaurants were open prior to my working with them, then the third opened later. They were a mess bookkeeping-wise. The biggest struggle they had was that the books weren't getting done until after the end of the month, even weeks after the fact. Bills were paid with manual checks each week based on what the vendors said was owed, and accounts payable was unknown. Plus, all the money was in one account, so they did not have any clarity on whether that was enough to cover payroll, sales tax, debt, and their true accounts payable. They were often short when it came time for payroll, and the monthly pull for sales taxes was always a big stressor since they didn't know where the funds to cover it would come from.

"The money would come in on Monday or Tuesday from the weekend credit card sales, and they would use it up before all their obligations were met... Parkinson's Law, live and in action. Then payroll would come due at the end of the week, and often there was not enough to cover it. All the usual issues we see when working with restaurants.

"Once we cleaned up the books and brought them current, we immediately set up Profit First. We got them on a system where their books were updated weekly, allocations were completed weekly, and bills were paid on time each week. Also, we set up their Profit First accounts slightly differently because each of the restaurants had ten-plus owners who were also the investors. So, instead of having Owner's Pay, Owner's Tax *and* Profit Accounts, we combined all three percentages into the profit allocation each week. The investors get a quarterly profit distribution until their initial investment is paid back, and after they are paid back, they will share in the profits. Doing it this way made the quarterly distribution super easy and consistent since it is already allocated to its own Profit Account, weekly.

"We also set up and utilize Sales Tax and Payroll Accounts. Doing this was extremely helpful to them right off the bat because they had everything separated out each week. This means there is a lot less stress around the times when payroll and sales tax come due. Having this money set aside every week, thus eliminating the fire drill of having to figure out where the funds will come from, has been like a giant weight being lifted from these operators.

"Another great benefit of implementing Profit First is, they always know how much they have in operating funds

(OPEX) to run the restaurants, and during the height of COVID, they never ran out of money. They had to dip into their Reserve Account a little, but they were able to stay open and strong the whole time. If we hadn't worked with them, gotten their books in order, and implemented Profit First, I don't think they would have made it through the pandemic."

CHAPTER 5

This Will Suck, but Do It Anyway

AT THIS POINT, YOU MIGHT think it's a good time to set the book aside until you're "ready" or in a different "mind frame." I strongly urge you to stay with me here. THIS IS AN EXTREMELY IMPORTANT CHAPTER. Whether you decide to give Profit First a try or think it's for the birds, the information you will get from completing the exercise in this chapter is very enlightening. That said, if you love math, numbers, and financial statements, then please go ahead and re-title this chapter "This Is My Favorite Chapter."

At the end, I will share Cassie's story with you. It's a true story, and although I changed her name, everything else is told exactly as it happened. And I can tell you this with 100% certainty: Had this book been around for Cassie to read early on, the story would have a very different ending. That's how strongly I feel about you reading this chapter and completing the exercise.

I'm going to teach you how to complete your Profit or "Instant" Assessment. The only difference between a Profit Assessment and an Instant Assessment is the level of detail used to create it. A full Profit Assessment can get into all the nitty-gritty detail, going back years, but we aren't going to do that here, nor is it necessary. Your Instant Assessment is all we need to get the job done. This extremely important assessment will tell us very clearly and distinctly where the money has gone in your restaurant. You might be thinking, *Out the door,* and you're probably right, but we want to get more specific than that. What we are going to determine in this Instant Assessment is how much of every dollar of income went toward your food and beverage vendors (COGS), payroll, profit, owner's pay, owner's tax, and operational expenses (OPEX). And when we divide each one of these totals by your gross income, we will get a percentage for each.

The way we do this is by reviewing your financials, your P&L and balance sheet reports. Then we use the numbers from these reports to complete your Instant Assessment and get to your CAPs ("current allocation percentages"). Don't have financials? Just grab your bank statements, credit card statements, or similar documents showing how the money moves through your business. This doesn't have to be perfect. We just want to get a good idea of where the money has been going.

You don't need an accountant or a bookkeeper to do this for you, although you can certainly ask! I am all about delegation. But there is no need to balance or reconcile accounts right now. As a matter of fact, if you are an accountant or bookkeeper or think like one, then you'll want to take that hat off. This exercise is a very simplified way of looking at money. Something

I find helpful with this exercise is to visualize piles of money. The first pile, all the money you brought in from sales, will be the biggest (hopefully). So just imagine that everyone paid you in cash and you threw it all in a big pile on the floor. That is your income as reported on your Instant Assessment. Now we start picking up handfuls of that cash and putting it into smaller piles based on how you spent it. We do this until there is no money left in your income pile. I really want you to envision this exercise in this way so that you don't start to get caught up in debits and credits and accruals and journal entries, AP (accounts payable) and AR (accounts receivable), and lions and tigers and bears. This is just old-school cash in and cash out.

I think Mike says it best in *Profit First* when he writes, "Profit First is a cash-management system. We don't do anything on accrual or any of that funny-money stuff. It is really simple: Did you get the cash or not? And did you spend the cash or not? That's it. Nothing else really matters unless cash happens. So that is why our focus is exclusively on cash. If you are wondering how Profit First addresses depreciation or accounts receivable (or inventory assets), you are still thinking funny money. We are only going to measure actual cash transactions. Money in. Money out. Real money. Period."[8]

The numbers may not be exact. This isn't an accounting exam and the numbers do not have to balance. We just want to get as close as we can to understanding what happens with the cash flowing through your restaurant.

Let's bust this out.

YOUR INSTANT ASSESSMENT

TO COMPLETE YOUR INSTANT ASSESSMENT, let's first get an understanding of what our goal is and how we are going to get there. To sum it up, pretty much all the "cash" in your restaurant, aside from meals or sales tax, belongs in one of the seven "piles" as described above in my visual of cash on the floor. Let's start calling them "buckets" from here on out, though, because using the word "pile" repeatedly just sounds weird. ("Cash" in this case is referring to all money from sales whether in the form of credit cards, cash, a third-party payment processor such as Venmo or PayPal, or gift cards)

INCOME BUCKET: This is your gross income/sales based on deposits for a specific period, usually one year, *less* all meals and sales tax paid. As we discussed in the previous chapter, meals and sales taxes are simply "pass-through" taxes and do not belong anywhere on your P&L. You collect these taxes from your customers and turn around and pay them to the appropriate government agency. They are neither income nor expense and have no place in your assessment.

BUCKET 1: COGS – This bucket represents the total paid for all food and beverage purchases during the same period as your Income Bucket.

BUCKET 2: PAYROLL – This bucket represents the total paid for all restaurant labor (payroll) during the same period as your Income Bucket, including management *but* excluding owner's pay and payments to office staff.

BUCKET 3: PROFIT – This bucket represents any profit distributions made and/or profit set aside for the period. This is actual cash money, not just an idea of the profit you think you made or a number at the bottom of your P&L. (Hint: Most restaurateurs enter zero dollars, but that may change as you finish this assessment. If this number ends up being negative, it most likely means that you have debt in your business that "funded" the loss.)

BUCKET 4: OWNER'S PAY – This is all money paid to the owners via salary or wages, draws or distributions, and any personal expenses paid on behalf of the owners through the business accounts. Look at your payroll and review the P&L to tally all personal expenses, i.e., car payments, personal insurances, personal meals, etc. Then look at your balance sheet under "Owner's Draws," "Member Draws," or "Shareholder Distributions" and add up all amounts paid to the owners during the same period as your Income Bucket.

BUCKET 5: OWNER'S TAX – This bucket represents the taxes paid on behalf of the owners *for the owners' personal tax liabilities*. This is not for sales or meals tax or for any business taxes. This bucket only represents amounts paid from the business accounts to cover the owners' personal taxes.

BUCKET 6: OPEX – This final bucket represents all other operating expenses of the business not mentioned or represented above. One quick way to get this total is to retrieve the "Total Expenses" line from your P&L and subtract all owner's pay and owner's expenses, such as the payments for the owner's personal vehicle or cell phone, that were included on that report.

To check your work, add up Buckets 1 through 6. They should total what's in your Income Bucket. If they do not, you either made an error and need to go back and check your math or you spent more money than you had in your Income Bucket. If that is the case, then the difference is a loss, or negative profit.

To figure out how much goes into each bucket, you will need the following reports run for one full year, calendar or fiscal, on a *cash basis only*. If you haven't been in business for a full year yet, no problem; simply run your reports for the number of months you have been in business and use that. If you haven't opened your restaurant yet, you can use your set of projections to run this exercise. If you don't have a set of projections, it's a good thing you have this book—keep reading. Here's what you need.

- Profit and loss standard report
- Profit and loss detail report
- Balance sheet

You also want to be sure that your P&L isn't insanely wrong. One way to figure this out, if you're not sure, is to review your

P&L *detail* report. This is a long report that lists all the income and expenses that make up your P&L. What you want to look for on this detail report is that all your food purchases are listed under "Cost of Goods Sold: Food Purchases," or however you have identified this category in your accounting software. The same goes for your beverage purchases, which should all be included under your "Cost of Goods Sold: Beverages," or however this category is named in your accounting software. Do this review for all the categories on your P&L just to ensure that all the transactions make sense and belong where they are.

If there are any personal expenses blended in with your operating expenses, you want to back them out of your OPEX total and add them to your Owner's Pay Bucket.

You then want to check your balance sheet to see if there was any activity under the "Equity" section that was personal pay taken out of the business and was not represented on your P&L for the same period (such activity is usually called "Owner's Draw/Distributions" or "Shareholder Distributions"). Add those amounts to your Owner's Pay Bucket. You may also find any profit distributions or taxes paid on the owner's behalf on your balance sheet. If so, please add those amounts to your Profit and Owner's Tax Buckets, respectively.

If you already know that you have a great set of books and reports you can trust, then your P&L standard report might look something like this:

Example: *Lucy's Bistro*

Restaurant Profit and Loss		
One Year		
	Total	
Income		
Sales		
Food		275,000.00
Liquor		100,000.00
Wine		100,000.00
Beer		20,000.00
N/A Beverages		5,000.00
Total Sales	$	500,000.00
Total Income	$	500,000.00
Cost of Goods Sold and Labor		
Cost of Goods Sold		
COGS – Food		90,000.00
COGS – Liquor		32,000.00
COGS – Wine		32,000.00
COGS – Beer		5,000.00
COGS – N/A Beverages		1,000.00
Total Cost of Goods Sold	$	160,000.00
Labor		
Kitchen Labor		55,000.00
Front of House Labor		25,000.00
Managers		75,000.00
Total Labor	$	155,000.00
Total Cost of Goods Sold and Labor	$	315,000.00
Gross Profit (RR)	$	185,000.00
Expenses		
Administrative Expenses		20,250.00
Advertising & Marketing		10,000.00
Direct Operating Expense		40,000.00
Occupancy Expense		50,000.00
Owners Pay & Personal Expenses		74,000.00
Total Expenses	$	194,250.00
Net Operating Income	–$	9,250.00
Net Income	–$	9,250.00

Using the chart below, fill in the total amounts in each box according to the above P&L standard report.

		ACTUAL $
Income Bucket	TOP LINE REVENUE/ GROSS SALES	$ 500,000.00
Bucket 1	COGS (FOOD, LIQ, BEV)	$ 160,000.00
Bucket 2	PAYROLL (EXCL. OWNER)	$ 155,000.00
	REAL REVENUE	$ 185,000.00
Bucket 3	PROFIT	$ (9,250.00)
Bucket 4	OWNER'S PAY	$ 74,000.00
Bucket 5	OWNER'S TAXES	$ —
Bucket 6	OPEX	$ 120,250.00

The final component to this exercise is to simply divide the amount in each Bucket, 1–6, by your Income Bucket to get your current allocation percentages (CAPs). Meaning, this is where you *currently* allocate every dollar that comes into your restaurant.

For example, in this chart, Lucy's Bistro had a total revenue of $500,000 and spent $160,000 on cost of goods sold (COGS). To calculate the COGS percentage for this example, divide $160,000 by $500,000 to get .32 or 32%.

Here is the completed chart with CAPs:

		ACTUAL $	CAPs %
Income Bucket	TOP LINE REVENUE/GROSS SALES	$ 500,000.00	100%
Bucket 1	COGS (FOOD, LIQ, BEV)	$ 160,000.00	32%
Bucket 2	PAYROLL (EXCL. OWNER)	$ 155,000.00	31%
	REAL REVENUE	$ 185,000.00	37%
Bucket 3	PROFIT	$ (9,250.00)	–5%
Bucket 4	OWNER'S PAY	$ 74,000.00	40%
Bucket 5	OWNER'S TAXES	$ –	0%
Bucket 6	OPEX	$ 120,250.00	65%

If I were discussing these CAPs with the owner of Lucy's, here is how I would describe them.

Your restaurant had $500,000 in gross sales last year. For every dollar that came in, $.32 went toward your COGS and $.31 went to cover your payroll. That left you with $.37 of every dollar to pay all your other expenses including owner's pay, tax, and profit.

So, if we take your gross sales of $500,000 and multiply that number by 37%, we will get the real revenue of $185,000.

$$\$500,000 \times 37\% = \$185,000.$$

Put another way, this $185,000 is what you have left to pay for all your operating expenses including rent, utilities, direct operating costs, office "stuff," professional fees, advertising, software, owner's pay, taxes, profit, etc.

When you tallied up your operating expenses, they totaled $120,250. If we subtract your operating expenses of $120,250 from your real revenue of $185,000, we get a balance of $64,750.

$$\$185,000 - \$120,250 = \$64,750.$$

But Lucy, you paid yourself $74,000 over this same time period via a salary, draws, and coverage of some personal expenses. If we subtract your owner's pay of $74,000 from your real revenue balance of $64,750, we arrive at a loss of –$9,250.

$$\$64,750 - \$74,000 = -\$9,250.$$

This amount goes into your Profit Bucket. Except it's negative, so it's the opposite of profit. It's more like a bucket with a hole in the bottom.

How do you end up with negative cash? That's usually where debt or investments kick in.

Here's another way to look at the same financials by using a checkbook register.

Number or Code	Date	Transaction Description	Payment, Fee, Withdrawal (–)	Deposit, Credit (+)	Balance $
Dept	12/31/21	Gross Sales Deposit		500,000	
					500,000
Check	12/31/21	COGS Purchases	160,000		
					340,000
Check	12/31/21	Payroll	155,000		
					185,000
Check	12/31/21	Owners Pay	74,000		
					111,000
Check	12/31/21	Operation Expenses	120,250		
				BALANCE	**–9,250**

Looking at it from this angle, you've just overdrawn your checking account!

Now what? You can't just leave your checking account with a negative balance. Imagine the fees! What do you do? You look to borrow money—fast—and probably from anyone who's willing to lend it to you at a high interest rate and with lots of fees. Or maybe you even borrow from yourself, and that isn't any better. Plowing your own money into a restaurant that is losing money without a plan to pay it back is simply enabling your business to continue to lose more money. No matter where it comes from, this is called debt. And while sometimes necessary, it is not your friend (more on this later). The only way to pay down and get rid of debt is through profit, which is what we are going to solve in this book.

Does any of this look or sound familiar to you? Have you ever found yourself in a place where you just couldn't pay everything that needed to be paid when it needed to be paid? At that point, you probably looked for a "short-term" cash infusion to get you through until that next Saturday night or busy season. Maybe this has happened more than once?

It's that vicious merry-go-round again: You just need more money so you can get to the next Saturday night, which leaves you still needing more money, which might mean taking on more debt until you get to that *next* Saturday night...

In Lucy's example above, we can stop that merry-go-round almost immediately. Now that we've completed the Instant Assessment, we know a few things about her restaurant.

1. The prime costs are 3% too high.
2. The OPEX percentage is too high.
3. If Lucy can find ways to lower her COGS by just 2% and her payroll by 1% and look for cost-cutting opportunities in her operational expenses while *simultaneously* beginning to take her profit first, she can turn this ship around pretty quickly.

But not everyone is as lucky as Lucy.

PROFIT FIRST CAUTIONARY TALE

Cassie's Burger Shack

THROUGHOUT THIS BOOK, YOU WILL read about so many great benefits of Profit First. I uncover new ones all the time. Sometimes, though, the benefits are disguised as problems. Big problems.

Take the case of Cassie's Burger Shack. Cassie, the owner, came to me after reading *Profit First*. She was fired up about the possibility of implementing the system at her restaurant. She, like so many, knew it could be a game-changer for her business.

When I met with Cassie, she was beyond excited to get started. I asked her to send me an invitation to access her QuickBooks Online file so I could review her numbers, history, etc. And as is usually the case, the numbers weren't right. Accounts were not being reconciled properly. Her chart of accounts was inaccurate, so she wasn't focusing on the right numbers—or any numbers, for that matter.

Cassie operated like so many other restaurateurs I encounter. She lived for the busy days and treaded water on the other days, then held her breath until the next busy day came along. There was no time to study financials or understand the numbers. She operated in a constant cycle of working just to keep the doors open for another day.

Eager to get started, Cassie had already set up her Profit First bank accounts before we began to work together. This was great, except we still needed to complete her Profit Assessment, and before we could do that, we needed to clean up her books. I am not one to dampen anyone's excitement, so since she had already opened these accounts, I told her to go ahead and transfer 1% of her deposits over to the Profit Account while we worked to remodel her books.

As you learned earlier in this chapter, understanding where all your dollars have gone historically is how we get to your starting point, your current allocation percentages or CAPs. Upon completing Cassie's Profit Assessment, a giant red flag presented itself. First, her combined food and beverage cost was 50%. This number should be closer to 30%. That was 20% we needed to find and lower. Tough, but doable.

The next red flag we came across was in her OPEX or operational expenses. This amount came to 113% of her real revenue. The number should be closer to 30%, which meant we needed to find 83% worth of savings. That would be a very tall order; it would take some time and possibly some soul-searching. But again, almost anything is possible.

The third red flag was that Cassie wasn't paying herself. And when I say not paying herself, she was taking home under $20,000 a year as her owner's pay for working full-time and then some, which is a non-livable wage in most places in the US.

The fourth red flag we found was the killer, and that is how she "funded" the losses her restaurant suffered on a regular basis. You see, when you view a loss, a negative number at the bottom of your P&L (sometimes it's in red), this negative number is important to note. It doesn't just come out of nowhere like a bad report card. That loss you see had to be funded—otherwise, how would you have been able to spend 113% on operating expenses, for example? That 113% means that you spent all your income, 100%, and then another 13% on top of that. Where did that money come from? It could only come from a decrease in cash (a lowered bank account balance), an increase in accounts payable (credit), and/or debt. Cassie's bank account often went as low as one could go and she was behind on paying her vendors. *And* she also had several very high-interest loans. But Cassie's Burger Shack was not making a profit to service these loans, so to make payments, she had to obtain more debt.

To summarize, she had to take out loans to cover the losses from her restaurant operations. And because she continued to operate at a loss, she could not make the required loan payments. But the loans had to be paid, which meant there was less cash to pay expenses, which then required Cassie to incur more debt in order to pay those expenses. This is a cyclone of hell. And without profit, you can never get out of it. Somehow, Cassie's Burger Shack had functioned like this for many years.

The end of this story includes some good news and some bad news.

By implementing Profit First, we were able to bring profitability to Cassie's Burger Shack. It took a few months and a lot of work, but in the end, she was able to turn a small profit.

The bad news was that she had already dug a hole so deep with debt because of years of operating at a loss that we knew she would never climb out of it. At least not in one lifetime.

Cassie's Burger Shack shut down for good six months after we began working together. That's the bad news.

But the good news is, we stopped the bleeding. Prior to implementing Profit First, Cassie could not see the forest for the trees. She had that common restaurateur mindset that if she just worked hard enough and could manufacture as many Saturday nights as possible, all would eventually be well. It would not. Not in this case. Implementing Profit First, and immediately seeing and understanding where every dollar was going and why there was never enough, showed us the writing on the wall: This business was broken. Cassie had to make the very difficult yet very necessary decision to close the restaurant. This stopped the bleeding, stopped her relentless pursuit to make every night a Saturday night, and stopped her from metaphorically pulling her hair out because she could never get ahead.

Cassie went on to become a nutritionist who specializes in helping people with celiac disease and is living her best life.

To Cassie, it may have felt at the time that this industry chewed her up and spit her out, but she is absolutely better for it now. Everything feels easier, lighter, and less intense, and she is grateful to be free of that never-ending cycle of never winning.

Owning a restaurant is an education in hustle, hard work, and perseverance like no other. And sometimes, no matter how hard you hustle, you can't always get the results that you want—especially if the numbers don't work.

If Cassie had known about Profit First just a couple of years earlier, maybe even just a year earlier, there might have been a different ending to this story. I know this would have been true for my restaurant. And now that you're here, we're about to rewrite your story as well.

Let's keep going.

"WHEN YOU HAVE MADE AS MANY MISTAKES AS I HAVE THEN YOU CAN BE AS GOOD AS ME."

Wolfgang Puck

CHAPTER 6

This Is How You Will Use the System

AT THIS POINT, YOU MAY or may not have attempted to complete your Instant Assessment. I'm guessing that either curiosity got the best of you and you gave it a shot, or you're just reading straight through and will get back to that later. If Cassie's story from the last chapter resonates with you at all, or if you are just unsure whether your restaurant is truly profitable or not, I strongly suggest that you stop reading now and go complete your Instant Assessment. At least give it your best attempt and then ask for help from a professional if you need it. Because no matter what you find, no matter what comes to light, simply knowing is half the battle. The other half is how to fix it. And that's exactly what we're going to do.

One of my closest friends used to own a restaurant on the Upper East Side of Manhattan. Like so many small, independent restaurants, it struggled. I remember one day we were having a conversation about it, and she said, "You know, Kasey, when your restaurant just keeps losing money, at some point, it doesn't really matter how much." She said this in jest, but I knew where she was coming from, which is denial. If your restaurant is losing money, you want to know this as soon as humanly possible and fix it. Stop the bleeding and start recovering. Every minute, every hour, every day matters.

For the purposes of this chapter, we will use the restaurant financials from Lucy's Bistro in Chapter 5 as your example Instant Assessment. However, if you did complete or attempt an Instant Assessment for your own restaurant, awesome! You will want to have it handy as you go through this exercise, and when we're done, you will be ready to rock and roll.

In this chapter, we turn your Instant Assessment into a road map with a starting point, CAPs (current allocation percentages), and a destination, TAPs (target allocation percentages). The difference between the two is called "the bleed." This represents where the money is bleeding out of your restaurant.

As restaurateurs, we are no strangers to blood. From broken glasses to sharp knives, rarely does a night go by when someone isn't bleeding from a cut they endured before, during, or post-service. Because we know this to be true, there is a first aid kit in every restaurant and most managers and sous chefs have become amateur EMTs over the years. Without a well-stocked first aid kit and people on staff who know what to do, blood can get pretty scary and possibly derail an entire service.

The same is true for your finances. Without a plan, without intention, and without a system to organize your money, the money will continue to bleed out of your restaurant.

Your Instant Assessment is the diagnosis of how and where to stop the bleeding. MacDaddy PF Cash is your long-lasting cure.

Let's get started.

CHARTING YOUR COURSE TO PROFIT

HERE IS ANOTHER LOOK AT the Instant Assessment for Lucy's Bistro that you will use in the absence of your own Instant Assessment.

Your CAPs (current allocation percentages) are your starting point. This is where you are now.

Your goal is to get to TAPs (target allocation percentages) as shown in the chart below. This is your destination.

TAPs CHART	A	B	C	D	E
Gross Revenue	$0– 625K	$625K– 1.25M	$1.25M– 2.5M	$2.5M– 12.5M	$12.5M– 25M
Less COGS ~ 30%	$187,500	$375,000	$750,000	$3,750,000	$7,500,000
Less Labor ~ 30 %	$187,500	$375,000	$750,000	$3,750,000	$7,500,000
Equals Real Revenue	$250,000	$500,000	$1,000,000	$5,000,000	$10,000,000
Real Revenue	**$0– 250K**	**$250K– 500K**	**$500K– 1M**	**$1M– 5M**	**$5M– 10M**
Profit	5%	10%	15%	10%	15%
Owner's Pay	50%	35%	20%	10%	5%
Owner's Taxes	15%	15%	15%	15%	15%
OPEX	30%	40%	50%	65%	65%

With a real revenue of $185,000, your TAPs fall under Column A. That shows your COGS and payroll each at 30% of gross revenue, and your profit at 5%, owner's pay at 50%, owner's tax at 15%, and OPEX at 30% of *real revenue*. These TAPs are where you want each dollar to go.

If you put your CAPs beside your TAPs, as in the chart below, you can see how far you are from reaching your TAPs in the column titled "The Bleed."

		ACTUAL $	CAPs %	TAPs %	PF $	THE BLEED	THE FIX
Income Bucket	TOP LINE REVENUE/ GROSS SALES	$ 500,000	100%	100%	$ 500,000		
Bucket 1	COGS (FOOD, LIQ, BEV)	$ 160,000	32%	30%	$ 150,000	$ (10,000)	Decrease COGS
Bucket 2	PAYROLL (EXCL. OWNER)	$ 155,000	31%	30%	$ 150,000	$ (5,000)	Decrease Payroll
	REAL REVENUE	$ 185,000	37%	40%	$ 200,000	$ 15,000	Increased RR
Bucket 3	PROFIT	$ (9,250)	−5%	5%	$ 10,000	$ 19,250	Increase Profit
Bucket 4	OWNER'S PAY	$ 74,000	40%	50%	$ 100,000	$ 26,000	Increase Owner's Pay
Bucket 5	OWNER'S TAXES	$ —	0%	15%	$ 30,000	$ 30,000	Increase Owner's Taxes
Bucket 6	OPEX	$ 120,500	65%	30%	$ 60,000	$ (60,250)	Decrease OPEX

"The Bleed" column shows us, in dollar amounts, how far off you are in each category. For example, as mentioned in the previous chapter, your prime costs are 3% too high, which equates to a $15,000 annual loss: $10,000 in COGS and $5,000 in payroll. We will go over ways to fix that in the next few chapters.

However, your larger task is going to be reducing OPEX so you can increase your allocations to profit, owner's pay, and owner's tax. This will not happen overnight, but it will happen over time and by making the right day-to-day choices that move you toward your TAPs. We'll explore ways you can reduce your OPEX in Chapter 9, but first, let's go over the practical application of how to move the money and get this party started.

MOVING THE MONEY

First, I will show you how moving money among your bank accounts will look from a *functional* viewpoint. After that, we will dig into the meat and potatoes of how you can make this happen from a *practical* viewpoint.

Prior to Profit First and MacDaddy PF Cash, your online banking screen when logging in to your account may have looked something like this:

Welcome to Bank of Money USA!		
		Current Balance:
Account ***123	Restaurant Checking	$ 12,846.21

That $12,846.21 is all the money your restaurant currently has. This is the amount you have with which to pay your vendors; make payroll; and cover rent, utilities, operating expenses, debt payments, meals tax, owner's pay, profit, owner's taxes, etc. Who do you pay first? And how much? If you're like many restaurateurs, or like I was when I operated my restaurants, then the phrase "the squeaky wheel gets the grease" comes into play here. Or basically, whoever yells the loudest or is the most annoying gets paid first. (I hesitate to use the descriptor "annoying"—they very reasonably just want to get paid for whatever they provided you—but you know who I mean.) By using the old bank balance accounting "system" to pay bills, you drain this account fast, most likely before all your obligations are met—and, I bet, before any profit is set aside.

When you use MacDaddy PF Cash, your online banking screen when logging in to your account will look something like this:

Welcome to Bank of Money USA!

		Current Balance:
Account ***123	Income Account	$ 12,846.21
Account ***000	Meals Tax Account (7)	$ 0.00
Account ***234	COGS Checking Account (31)	$ 0.00
Account ***345	Payroll Checking Account (30)	$ 0.00
Account ***456	Profit Account (1)	$ 0.00
Account ***567	Owners Pay Account (40)	$ 0.00
Account ***678	Owners Tax Account (1)	$ 0.00
Account ***789	OPEX Account (58)	$ 0.00

If you have an existing restaurant, chose to keep the same bank, and just added the additional bank accounts, then you may have decided to keep your current OPEX Account. In that case, there may be a balance in that account. That's fine. You can either leave it there or transfer it to your Income Account and then allocate it to all the other accounts from there.

There is no right or wrong way to handle any balance you have prior to implementing this system. That choice is up to you and whatever is going on financially with your restaurant at that time. If you need your full balance to pay vendors, payroll, etc., then perhaps you leave it in your OPEX Account or transfer it to your Payroll Account for that purpose. Or, if you're feeling caught up with vendors and payroll and you'd like to see what this thing is going to look like, then go ahead and move the balances you have in any existing accounts to your new Income Account. Then, allocate (transfer) according to your new MacDaddy PF Cash system. This choice is yours, and we are not taking any money away from you or your restaurant, so please don't be nervous about that. All the money will still be there, we are just giving every dollar a job by allocating it to a predetermined, nicknamed account.

When I say "allocate," I mean the same as "transfer" from a technical standpoint. Thus, when you are logged in to your bank online and ready to allocate funds from your Income Account to your other accounts, you will make transfers from the Income Account to the other accounts. I prefer to use the word "allocate" instead of "transfer" because allocating sounds like it is done with intention, while transferring just sounds mechanical. But for the purposes of this book and MacDaddy PF Cash, allocating and transferring are the same task.

On the above illustration of your online bank accounts, the numbers in parentheses to the right of each account name are the allocation percentages you are currently using (CAPs). While you do not have to add these numbers as part of your account nicknames, it can be helpful to have that information right there on the screen in front of you. And it is easy enough to edit or change your account nicknames on most banks' web platforms, so when it is time to adjust the percentages, you can quickly and easily make changes to the nicknames. I find this convenient because all the information you need to make the allocations is right there in front of you on one screen. Also, viewing these percentages right next to your actual dollar amounts can be very motivating and help you make the changes needed to move toward your TAPs. On the other hand, if you are unable to add the CAPs to your bank account nicknames, you will simply use your Instant Assessment to view those percentages while making your allocations.

The first allocation you'll make is to the Meals/Sales Tax Account. In our illustration, the current allocation percentage for meals tax is 7%; therefore, you allocate 7% of your deposit income to your Meals Tax Account.

The next allocations you will make are for your prime costs. As we determined in your Instant Assessment, your restaurant is running a little high at 32% COGS and 31% payroll. You think you can already do better by making a couple of immediate, small adjustments to COGS and payroll, so you're going to start your CAPs at 31% COGS and 30% payroll. Here is what your online banking screen will look like after you make those allocations:

	Welcome to Bank of Money USA!		
			Current Balance:
Account ***123	Income Account	$	4,659.32
Account ***000	Meals Tax Account (7)	$	899.23
Account ***234	COGS Checking Account (31)	$	3,703.56
Account ***345	Payroll Checking Account (30)	$	3,584.09
Account ***456	Profit Account (1)	$	0.00
Account ***567	Owners Pay Account (40)	$	0.00
Account ***678	Owners Tax Account (1)	$	0.00
Account ***789	OPEX Account (58)	$	0.00

The remaining balance in your Income Account, of $4,659.32, is your real revenue. Based on your Instant Assessment and using your CAPs, you make the appropriate allocations to the remaining accounts *in this order* (remember, order matters!): 1% to your Profit Account, 40% to Owner's Pay, 1% to Owner's Tax, and 58% to OPEX.

Here's what your banking screen will look like after you make those allocations:

	Welcome to Bank of Money USA!	
		Current Balance:
Account ***123	Income Account	$ 0.00
Account ***000	Meals Tax Account (7)	$ 899.23
Account ***234	COGS Checking Account (31)	$ 3,703.56
Account ***345	Payroll Checking Account (30)	$ 3,584.09
Account ***456	Profit Account (1)	$ 46.59
Account ***567	Owners Pay Account (40)	$ 1,863.73
Account ***678	Owners Tax Account (1)	$ 46.59
Account ***789	OPEX Account (58)	$ 2,702.41

That wasn't so bad, was it? All the money is still there, we just organized it a little differently and gave every dollar a job to do. Now, with the money spread out more than you may be used to, and especially if you tend to run tight with cash flow, this may make you a little nervous. After all, you don't have that big platter of just one account to feed everyone from anymore. That big platter may have been giving you a false sense of security along with no direction for how to manage the money. Now you have some guardrails up, and some guidance on where you should be focusing your improvement efforts. And now that you have all your accounts set up and are making your allocations, it's perfectly okay to practice bank balance accounting and check your accounts regularly or as often as you need to. In fact, it's encouraged! What this system has done is create a live, working budget for you to follow and manage.

At gross annual sales of $500,000 for Lucy's Bistro, the $12,846.21 in your Income Account used for this example would most likely represent about one week's sales. And given that you were already pretty close to your prime cost targets, you should feel pretty good about the balances in your COGS and Payroll Accounts. You may just need to keep an eye on those accounts to be sure those costs fall in line this week.

At this point, your Profit and Owner's Tax Accounts act more like savings accounts in which you set money aside for a quarter or more, and with just 1% being allocated to each, there's no need to worry too much here.

Your Owner's Pay Account is tracking with what you have been accustomed to taking as your pay per your Instant Assessment, and that allocation percentage has not changed, so, status quo here.

Finally, we come to your OPEX Account. With a balance of $2,702.41, you might be thinking it's a bit tight. I hear you. But remember, we've already taken care of your prime costs and owner's pay, so this amount is used for the other "stuff" that it takes to run a restaurant. Based on the sales associated with this balance, $2,702.41 should be enough to cover your operational expenses (OPEX) for the week. Again, we're going to deep-dive into these expenses in the next couple of chapters, so stay with me.

OUT OF SIGHT, OUT OF MIND

ONCE YOU HAVE COMPLETED ALL your allocations, bringing your Income Account to zero, there are two final allocations to be made using the remote savings accounts that you set up at a separate online bank.

All you need to do here is to log in to your remote savings bank and initiate two transfers. The first will be from your local Profit Account to your remote Profit Savings Account, and the second will be from your local Owner's Tax Account to your remote Tax Savings Account.

Here's what it might look like. This first illustration shows your bank balances as soon as you have completed your initial MacDaddy PF Cash allocations.

	Welcome to Bank of Money USA!		
		Current Balance:	
Account ***123	Income Account	$ 0.00	
Account ***000	Meals Tax Account (7)	$ 899.23	
Account ***234	COGS Checking Account (31)	$ 3,703.56	
Account ***345	Payroll Checking Account (30)	$ 3,584.09	
Account ***456	Profit Account (1)	$ 46.59	*Transfer*
Account ***567	Owners Pay Account (40)	$ 1,863.73	
Account ***678	Owners Tax Account (1)	$ 46.59	*Transfer*
Account ***789	OPEX Account (58)	$ 2,702.41	

This second illustration shows the zero balances in your Profit Account and your Owner's Tax Account after you have transferred those balances to their respective remote savings accounts.

Welcome to Bank of Money USA!

		Current Balance:	
Account ***123	Income Account	$	0.00
Account ***000	Meals Tax Account (7)	$	899.23
Account ***234	COGS Checking Account (31)	$	3,703.56
Account ***345	Payroll Checking Account (30)	$	3,584.09
Account ***456	Profit Account (1)	$	0.00
Account ***567	Owners Pay Account (40)	$	1,863.73
Account ***678	Owners Tax Account (1)	$	0.00
Account ***789	OPEX Account (58)	$	2,702.41

And this final illustration shows the allocations tucked away nice and neat, out of sight and out of mind, and earning a little interest.

Welcome to Remote Online Savings Bank!

		Current Balance:	
Account ***333	Profit Savings Account	$	46.59
Account ***666	Tax Savings Account	$	46.59
Account ***999	Reserve Savings Account	$	0.00

You will continue to allocate your profit and owner's tax to these remote savings accounts for a full quarter. At the end of each quarter, you will then do the reverse. Here's how this works:

1. If you are debt-free, great! Now you get to build the asset of your own "line of credit" or "rainy-day fund."

What I recommend is taking 50% of the profit that has accumulated in your Profit Savings Account over the quarter and moving that over to your new Reserve Funds Savings Account. Continue to do this every quarter to allow that Reserve Funds Savings Account to grow. It may take a little while for you to see a substantial or meaningful balance in that account, but it will happen, and without you realizing it. You will just follow the system, allocate the money, and work on improvements in your restaurant so that you can move toward your TAPs, and before you know it, everything will start to fall into place. Your prime costs will improve, your OPEX will improve, and because of these improvements your restaurant will run better and more smoothly, everyone including you will be happier, and so on. The benefits are real.

One day you will log in to your remote savings bank to make some allocations and, lo and behold, you will see a nice, fat balance in that Reserve Funds Savings Account—and you will sit back and wonder how you did it. Feel free to give yourself a pat on the back, because this is some good stuff happening. The Reserve Funds Savings Account is literally just that: your cash reserve to use in case of emergencies, to get you through any unforeseen challenges or cash shortages, to invest in your business, or maybe to use for expansion. Now you have that cushion that you may have heard others speak of but has always been a foreign concept to you. This cushion allows you some breathing room, some comfort, and some confidence, which can be very inspiring.

With this newfound confidence, you may notice some changes in the way you lead your business. Your vision for how you want your restaurant to perform and be received may come into clearer focus, and you may find yourself spending more time on the "higher level" or, dare I say, "important" stuff that really makes your restaurant shine because you aren't bogged down anymore, or certainly not as much. And at this point, you may no longer be in that cycle of the constant search for Saturday night. Thus, while the profit allocation amount in our example is quite low at $46.59, I can tell you with certainty that this $46.59 represents so much more than you may think. Stick with me and you'll see what I mean.

Next, transfer the remaining 50% in your Profit Savings Account back to your local Profit Account and use it as you wish. Some restaurateurs use some of this quarterly profit to reward managers or leadership; some use it to fund a reward for their staff or a company culture initiative; and others take it for their personal use, as the reward that it is for operating a great, profitable restaurant. It's your profit, you earned it, you decide.

2. On the other hand, if you have debt in your restaurant, you most certainly aren't alone. You do want to break free of debt, though, sooner rather than later. Therefore, I recommend moving just 5% or 10% from your Profit Savings Account to your Reserve Funds Savings Account and then transferring the balance back to your local Profit Account each quarter. From here, you will use this profit

to pay down debt. That might mean moving it one more time, into your OPEX Account, so that you can pay your debtors from there. Or, if you pay your debts online, you may be able to link your Profit Account to your debt service and pay it directly that way.

I recommend using your OPEX Account for this just to keep things clean and streamlined, as this is the account that is used to pay the restaurant's expenses (aside from prime costs) and will most likely (hopefully) always have a balance in it. Your Profit Account will mainly hold a zero balance, as it used to pass allocations to and from, so linking it with any expense or other debtor account may not be a great idea. And in the unlikely event that a fee is assessed, or something of that nature, your Profit Account may be in jeopardy of having a negative balance and thus incurring bank fees. We will dive further into the concept of debt, what it really is and how to manage it, in a later chapter.

3. Your Tax Savings Account is more straightforward. The purpose of this account is to pay the owner's tax liabilities now that you are running a profitable business. Therefore, at the end of each quarter, you will simply transfer the money that has accumulated in your remote Tax Savings Account back to your local Owner's Tax Account. You will use your local Owner's Tax Account to make your quarterly estimated tax payments to the IRS and your state where applicable. You may also use this account when you're ready to pay your final, annual taxes once your

business and personal tax returns are completed by your CPA. We will dive into more tax implication-type stuff in Chapter 11 but for now, let me just say this: Whether you are on salary, take a paycheck, or have not historically had much of a tax burden, you will still very much need and use this account. Again, more on this topic later, in Chapter 11.

THE STORY YOU SEE

AND THERE YOU HAVE IT. This is how you move the money. I know it just took me about fifteen pages to explain it, but it's going to take you less than ten minutes to complete this task. Log in, calculate your allocations (using the free MacDaddy PF Cash Calculator waiting for you at www.profitfirst4restaurants. com and click on "Tools"), make the transfers, and you're done. Now your money has intention and purpose, and so do you. Now you can focus on the areas of your restaurant that *need* focusing on. This is how you stop the bleeding.

The way the money moves through a business tells a story, and it's an important one. However, most entrepreneurs are too busy, too caught up in all the things, or even too scared to stop and really see what the numbers are telling them. With Profit First, and with MacDaddy PF Cash for restaurateurs, the story is being told right in front of your eyes every time you log in and make these allocations. You can't miss it! Based on the balances in your accounts, you will know almost instantaneously if your prime costs or operational expenses are too high or if your income was just too low for a given period. And you can make the necessary adjustments right away.

For example, one of the many benefits of using this system is knowing immediately that if you didn't hit your sales goal for a specific period, your payroll might be too high or higher than the allocation that you just made. You may have planned and scheduled for a busy night or weekend, but perhaps it was not as busy as you had hoped. You will need to move more money into your Payroll Account to cover that payroll sweep. Where will you take the money from? You probably can't take it from your COGS or OPEX Accounts; those vendors still need to be paid since you have already incurred those expenses. That leaves just the Profit, Owner's Pay, and Owner's Tax Accounts. Without Profit First and MacDaddy PF Cash, this is most likely where the money would come from to support that payroll, without you even realizing it, and you'd end up either not paying yourself what you should or using up your profits or both.

But now that choice is clear as day and right in front of you. What's it gonna be? There is no shame in having to plow profit and owner's pay back into your business when times are tough and cash is tight. We have all been there. But there is a significant difference when you are consciously making this decision and visually seeing the results, for example, when your Profit Account balance goes down so your Payroll Account balance can go up. The act of having to reduce your Profit Account so you can cover your payroll can be very motivating. This isn't a task you want to have to do all the time; thus, you may find yourself paying more attention to your scheduling and staffing so you won't have to take from profit or anywhere else the next time you make your allocations. And that's exactly where your attention should be, according to the numbers and the story they are telling you.

You are being intentional with your money so that you can be intentional with your time and attention. This is a recipe for success.

PROFIT FIRST SUCCESS STORY

Prep Kitchen, CA

PREP KITCHEN IS A HEALTHY, fast casual establishment that was only open a few months before they contacted us for help. The owners, young and fit and all-in on a healthy lifestyle, opened near their gym where they were sure to have a dedicated audience. This is their first foray into the restaurant industry, and it has been quite the learning experience. They didn't know what they didn't know and began reading any business book they could get their hands on. One of those books was *Profit First*, and that is how we met.

When my team began working with Prep Kitchen, we organized and structured their bookkeeping so that we had good numbers to work with when completing their Profit Assessment. The results were quite striking for the owners. Their biggest eye-popping moment early on was realizing the true cost of their takeout supplies and containers. Because Prep Kitchen is a fast casual establishment where all menu items are served in takeout containers, this was a large expense that they had not considered when costing their menu.

After their assessment, their focus was mainly on rehabbing their menu in such a way that they could incorporate somewhat substantial pricing increases without it appearing as though they'd just added two or three dollars to every item. Had they not put genuine thought into how to restructure their menu in a way that wouldn't shock and alienate their current guests, making the necessary changes could have been a public relations nightmare.

With the new menu launched and their payroll somewhat in line (both owners were the primary employees), their next task was to complete the expense analysis (you will learn about this in Chapter 9). Because this restaurant was relatively new, it was not bogged down with a ton of expenses it didn't need. While the exercise of performing an expense analysis can be the true benefit, there wasn't much to cut or trim, so their financial turnaround was largely dependent on their new menu pricing.

When Prep Kitchen first came to us, they had about $35,000 in the bank and owed about $57,000 in payables and credit cards. Plus, they were running at a loss of $143,000 on sales of $455,000. Yikes.

After about a year of implementing and fine-tuning MacDaddy PF Cash, they had $53,000 in their bank accounts, no payables or credit card debt, and a profit of $32,000 on sales of $895,500. There is still some work to be done as they move toward their TAPs, but I have no doubt that they'll get there.

Prep Kitchen, CA	Before PF	After PF
Bank Balance	$35,157	$52,849
Accounts Payable	$48,697	$0
Net Income/Profit	($143,645)	$32,059

"LUCK IS NOT A BUSINESS MODEL."

Anthony Bourdain [10]

CHAPTER 7

This Is Where Your Restaurant Fits In

I'D LIKE TO TAKE YOU through another exercise. Don't worry, no need for spreadsheets, financial reports, or math with this one. I just want you to think back to when you first envisioned your restaurant. Or, if that's a hazy memory, just imagine what a perfectly executed service looks like to you. And if you're at the stage where you're about to open your restaurant for the first time, or thinking about opening a restaurant, then I want you to close your eyes and really conceptualize what your restaurant will look and feel like through both your eyes and your guests'. See if you can tap into the "why" that brought you to this industry in the first place, and what you intended to achieve by having your own restaurant. No, this is not some kind of hypnosis, woo-woo mind trick, or vision board exercise, although I am not against any of those things. I just want you to imagine your restaurant at its best. There is a method to my madness here, so stick with me.

Depending on what side of the line you're on—the front of the house or the back—that image may be of the concept or décor, or it may be of the food and menu. Or maybe it's both.

While you're at it, I want you to envision how a typical night might work. My guess is that you might see waitstaff and a busser or two coiffed and dressed in clean, pressed uniforms. Maybe you see a host with a bright smile and warm greeting, or maybe that's you. There could be a bartender holding court at a full bar while maintaining the service bar. Perhaps you notice a food runner, dressed in black, gliding among the tables and delivering gorgeous, temperature-appropriate dishes to your enamored patrons. Smiles all around.

In the kitchen, you may see the chef at the helm in their crisp, clean chef's coat, conducting the night's service like the leader of a happy French brigade. Lots of voices calling out "Yes, Chef," or "Oui, Chef" while the sous chef, line cooks, pastry chef, garde-manger, dishwashers and whoever else *you* envision working in your kitchen are bustling about.

Maybe there's a valet, maybe not. Perhaps you have someone in the coat check or maybe someone in the office answering calls, taking reservations or takeout orders.

Now take a step back and into your guest's shoes, from the moment they pull up to or walk in your front door. I want you to visually travel with them through the restaurant. What do they see, hear, smell? What do your tables look like? What's on them? What kind of water service do you offer? What do your menus look like? How does the staff first approach the table? Are they selling or just taking orders? What happens once the order has been entered into your point-of-sale?

And from this point, I want you to think about what happens behind the scenes. Once the order is received, who makes it?

How do they make it? Are they making it inside their stations that they lovingly prepped and stocked prior to service? Or are they running around like chickens with their heads cut off trying to pull it together? How long does it take? Is everything being served consistently in every aspect—size, taste, shape, temperature?

Now it's the end of the night. Tables are cleared, checks are dropped, dishwashers are humming, glasses and service stations are getting restocked, the kitchen is being scrubbed from top to bottom, and the manager is beginning to cash out the servers and bartenders. Lights go up, the music shuts off, and some version of "You don't have to go home but you can't stay here" is whispered or shouted out to the remaining guests. Another service comes to a close.

Now I want you to take this same exercise and play it from the beginning, but this time, add dollar signs and dollar amounts to everything you see. That's right, add a "$____" to each of the moving pieces in your story. The dollar amount on your guest is your "check average," or what you anticipate a typical guest might spend in your restaurant. All the staff you encounter, from the front of the house to the back of the house to even yourself, should wear a dollar sign and figure representing what each person gets paid for that service. The tool your guests use to make a reservation, whether through OpenTable, another reservation service, or simply by phone or text, should have a figure on it to represent what you pay to utilize that service.

Now consider the menus, candles, linens, place settings, uniforms, service tools (i.e., wine keys, bottle openers, pens, notepads, mini-flashlights, check presenters, etc.). Give them all dollar signs and amounts. Maybe there are flowers or mints at the host stand; put dollar amounts on those too. Every drink you serve, every dish you sell should have a dollar sign and amount on it that represents your cost, what you paid for each item. Then do the same as you walk through your kitchen. There's a dollar sign and number on each member of the kitchen staff; the unused food in the walk-ins, in low-boys, and on the shelves; the paper in the dupe printer; tin foil, plastic wrap, take-out boxes and supplies, doilies—you get my drift. And this is *your* restaurant, so you can add and take away dollar signs and change their corresponding amounts according to what makes sense to you and your perfect service.

I know I said there wouldn't be any math with this exercise, and I meant it! But if you were to replay this story with the dollar signs and amounts now in place and jot down each figure, the equation might look something like this:

Guest Check Average – Food and Beverage Costs – Staff Payroll – (proportionate) OPEX Expenses = Profit.

You would know by the outcome of this equation if you had a viable, profitable business.

This is your business model. It either works—makes money/is profitable—or it doesn't. Feel free to tinker with it! As a matter of fact, I believe that tinkering with it and making it better should be the primary focus of the owner. Sometimes I imagine the owner as a grand puppeteer, pulling the strings and putting on a great show. But that show has to make money. It must be profitable for the show to go on. *How* profitable is up to you and your business model.

When I talk about your business model throughout this chapter and the rest of the book, I am referring to the financial model created by this exercise. Some may call it projections or a pro forma budget. I don't care what you call it, but the question, the bottom line, is this: How do you plan to be profitable?

UNDERSTANDING AND EMBRACING YOUR BUSINESS MODEL

At about the same time I left the restaurant industry (my partners and I had sold the restaurant and were heading in different directions), I also gave birth to my first child. This was a clear definition of a new chapter in my life. I knew that I needed to work, but I didn't see how I could continue to work in the restaurant industry the way I had been working—very long, late hours, more than six days a week—and still be a new mom just trying to figure things out.

As I took stock of my current skill set and which of those skills could possibly transfer outside the industry, or at least outside working in some labor-intensive role, I realized that I was good with numbers. I was good with money. I had to be to keep my restaurant alive for as long as I did prior to the sale. I had to be incredibly creative with every dollar that came in and stretch it as far as I could just to keep the doors open, product coming in, and employees somewhat happy, or at least paid.

When you are put in a position like this, a "do-or-die"-type position where any wrong move could end in disaster, you become hyper-aware of everything and for me, that included a laser-focus on the way money moved through my business. I became obsessed with every dollar that came in and tried my hardest to turn each single dollar into ten dollars. Newsflash: Not possible.

But what I did learn from this tumultuous time was how money moved through a business and how to keep track of it in a way that showed me on a regular basis—daily, weekly, monthly—where the money was going. And if I could visually see where the money was going and understand basic restaurant accounting percentages of where the money *should* be going, i.e., 30% COGS, 30% labor, 15% occupancy, etc., I knew immediately where I was off—where I was bleeding. Was my food or beverage cost too high? Was the labor cost too high? Were occupancy, advertising, direct operating, meals and entertainment, dues, subscriptions, or any other expenses I tracked too high?

And how would I know if my expenses were too high, too low, or just right? I would know based on my business model. Every business has a business model. It's either the one you created deliberately or the one you created without realizing it.

HERE'S WHY A BUSINESS MODEL IS SO IMPORTANT

Let's take a 200-seat restaurant versus a 40-seat restaurant. If you had your choice and wanted to make money, which would you choose? One might think the 200-seat restaurant would make more money, but that is not necessarily true. It may gross more money (or maybe not), but that's a far cry from making more money. I mean, a 200-seat restaurant will presumably cost a lot more to run and staff. That's a *big* payroll, tons of inventory and probably a very high occupancy cost as well. Not to mention the stress of having to fill 200 seats every night! If you're smart, you won't build a business model that requires you to fill 200 seats per night. If you've got a room with 200 chairs and only 50 are taken, that's a lot of empty chairs. And those empty chairs make a very loud statement. Is there a way around this? Sure. But it all comes back to your business model.

Now, if it were up to me, I'd most likely go for the 40-seat restaurant and model the shit out of it. I'd model it so that my break-even was 10 seats a night and anything above was gravy—as they say. Or maybe a 20-seat break-even. Whatever. The point is, you've got to know your business model. And then you have to figure out how to make that model happen on a regular basis. And then you better it. And better it. And tweak it until your business model, your restaurant, is a lean, mean, money-making machine.

And you love every second of it because this is the hustle that pays off.

Let's go.

FIGURING OUT YOUR BUSINESS MODEL

THERE ARE A COUPLE OF different ways to look at this.

1. If you already have a business plan or have created financials for your restaurant that presumably showed a profit, then compare those projections to what you came up with on your Instant Assessment from Chapter 5. I assume your projections will look quite different than your Instant Assessment, but all you need to do is re-add some of the numbers on your projections so that they fit into the six buckets in Chapter 5: COGS, Payroll, Profit, Owner's Pay, Owner's Tax, and Operating Expenses. Then divide each bucket by your projected gross revenue to reveal what allocation percentages you projected. Because these were your projections, and assuming you plan on having a financially successful and profitable restaurant, then these, in essence, are your TAPs.

2. If you do not have projections, then your TAPs (see chart below) will simply act *as* your projections as described in #1 above. Reviewing the table below, these are the target percentages you want to hit based on your *real revenue*, NOT your gross revenue.

Let me explain.

In the TAPs chart that follows, I used the industry standard of 30% for COGS and 30% for payroll. Now, that said, let me be clear: These are *average* restaurant industry standards.

TAPs CHART	A	B	C	D	E
Gross Revenue	$0–625K	$625K–1.25M	$1.25M–2.5M	$2.5M–12.5M	$12.5M–25M
Less COGS *~ 30%*	$187,500	$375,000	$750,000	$3,750,000	$7,500,000
Less Labor *~ 30 %*	$187,500	$375,000	$750,000	$3,750,000	$7,500,000
Equals Real *Revenue*	$250,000	$500,000	$1,000,000	$5,000,000	$10,000,000
Real Revenue	**$0–250K**	**$250K–500K**	**$500K–1M**	**$1M–5M**	**$5M–10M**
Profit	5%	10%	15%	10%	15%
Owner's Pay	50%	35%	20%	10%	5%
Owner's Taxes	15%	15%	15%	15%	15%
OPEX	30%	40%	50%	65%	65%

Are there some restaurants that run a 22% COGS and 36% labor? Sure.

Are there some restaurants that run a 37% COGS and 24% labor? You betcha.

These numbers are not one-size-fits-all. But what we do have is *your* business model; the model that shows how you intend to be profitable. Think back to the exercise we did at the beginning of this chapter. When you designed your restaurant's menu, you had an idea of how much you would profit off each item. You also had an idea of who you would need in the kitchen, and on the floor, to execute these sales. Maybe you didn't write all this down or use a fancy spreadsheet with a solid business plan behind it. And while it never ceases to amaze me that people still go into business without a plan and basic projections, it happens all the time. Thank God you're here. Because whether you wrote a Nobel Prize-winning business plan, sketched it on the back of a cocktail napkin, or did absolutely nothing, we're going to fix your business model right now.

HOW TO MAKE IMPROVEMENTS TO MOVE TOWARD TAPs – GAME PLAN

LET'S TAKE THIS BUCKET BY bucket, from the top down, and discuss ways to cut and control your costs in order to move you toward your TAPs.

Once again, here is Lucy's Bistro's Instant Assessment to use as we go through this exercise.

Or, if you have completed your own Instant Assessment, you may want to have that handy as we go through the next few chapters.

		ACTUAL $	CAPs %
Income Bucket	TOP LINE REVENUE/GROSS SALES	$ 500,000.00	100%
Bucket 1	COGS (FOOD, LIQ, BEV)	$ 160,000.00	32%
Bucket 2	PAYROLL (EXCL. OWNER)	$ 155,000.00	31%
	REAL REVENUE	$ 185,000.00	37%
Bucket 3	PROFIT	$ (9,250.00)	−5%
Bucket 4	OWNER'S PAY	$ 74,000.00	40%
Bucket 5	OWNER'S TAXES	$ —	0%
Bucket 6	OPEX	$ 120,250.00	65%

Using our example of the Instant Assessment for Lucy's Bistro's, we can see that the COGS and payroll are a little high right off the bat. Not terrible, but there is definitely room for improvement. However, if Lucy was under the assumption that she was running at 25% COGS or 28% labor, now is the time to figure out where the leak is and plug it up. We will deep-dive into how to fix your prime costs in Chapter 8.

Next, we will analyze the operational expenses restaurants incur and discuss ways to control, trim back, and/or eliminate them. And I don't necessarily mean forever! This is an exercise in getting you back to your original business model, or getting you as close as possible to a new, profitable business model. Later, you may be able to build back in some expenses you trim or eliminate during this stage in the process. This is where we cut off the dead weight, the weight that may be holding you and your restaurant down. We will go deep into this exercise in Chapter 9.

This isn't a fire sale or even have the look of a "going out of business sale," nothing like that. This is simply paying attention to every dollar that leaves your business and asking yourself if your business could have lived without it *and* still delivered on your promise to your guests. If the answer is "Yes, we could live without it" then cut the expense. If the answer is no, then leave it and move on to the next expense. The bottom line is this: At the end of the day, if you say no—meaning that your restaurant could not live, could not deliver on its promise, without all the expenses incurred—and you're still operating at a loss, then your business model is broken.

Maybe it's broken from the sales side of the equation. Maybe your expenses are as low and lean as possible and you're still operating at a loss because you aren't selling enough to cover even your basic expenses. If this is the case, your task is clear. This may be the point where investment or debt makes sense. You now know that you need to improve sales, and you should have a very specific plan to make that happen. Whatever plan you determine will work best for your restaurant may come at an expense. You may need to borrow the money to execute this new sales plan. If your sales plan is specific and measurable, which it absolutely should be, then proceed, but proceed with caution. Have a detailed timeframe outlined with measurable results and targets to hit that make sense for the money you are investing.

Put guardrails up around your plan when using debt for growth. Debt is not free money. Quite the opposite. It's expensive money with strings attached. Thus, it needs to have a very specific, measurable use within a specific timeframe that creates profit. You need a plan to get it, a plan to use it, and a plan to pay it back. We will cover all things debt in Chapter 10.

Okay, so now you've got your business model. You know, or have a strong idea of, what your prime costs and operational expenses are or should be, what you pay yourself, and what your profit should look like.

Let's make it happen.

CHAPTER 8

This Is Where We Nail Your Prime Costs

I WORKED WITH A CHEF once who was very talented. He was one of *Food & Wine* magazine's top ten chefs in the country at that time and had won numerous other awards for his culinary skills as well. Because he was so talented, the owners of the restaurant we worked in let him have free rein with the menu. He changed it often, as often as the wind blows, some might say, and it kept people coming back to see what was new and fresh. Even Julia Child, among other celebrities, came to the restaurant to try his food. We had a long waiting list to reserve a table on the weekends and were busy every night of the week for a while. It was an exciting time for the chef, the owners, and everyone who worked at this little gem of a restaurant in Boston's South End.

I was the manager and did the bookkeeping. This is the place where I first learned to read and begin to understand the numbers. I vividly remember sitting at the makeshift desk in the basement "office" of the restaurant on a hot summer Monday morning with a stack of invoices from the week piled as high as my computer monitor. I would get such a feeling of accomplishment when I finally finished entering all those bills into our accounting software, filed them away, and was able to see my desktop again.

However, by the time I was done printing the checks to pay those vendors, I had drained the bank account. Sure, we made payroll, but the owners weren't on it. And we paid the rent. But by the time we paid all our vendors, there was nothing left in the bank account. Nothing left to show for having produced a very busy week and weekend. I was so perplexed by this that I started to dig into the numbers. I was only twenty-five years old, and accounting was not my strong suit, but I knew something just wasn't adding up. And the owners, as lovely as they were, were not numbers people either. They were visionaries! They had the vision to hire this young, extraordinarily talented chef and create a restaurant where people wanted to come and spend hours dining, trying this new, "exotic" food, and spending really good money doing it. These owners, like so many, just assumed that profitability would naturally follow. It did not.

I started my quest to find where the money went with the number one product we sold: food. I added up all the food purchases we made in a week. I then ran a report from the restaurant's POS (point-of-sale) computer to tally the food sales for that same week. I divided the total food purchases by the total food sales to see what our COGS percentage was for food. At this point in my career, and by participating in manager meetings, I knew that our food cost should run about 30%. Our chef was sure he was running closer to 28%. While I don't remember the exact amounts today, I do remember discovering that his food cost was over 40%. That's 10% higher than it should have been and what the owners assumed it was, and 12% higher than the chef thought it was. To make matters worse, most restaurants, if you're lucky, run a 10% profit margin. Since this food cost was 10% over average, it ate up the entire profit margin! No wonder there was no money left over after the bills were paid! Mystery solved.

I wish it were that easy. While the mystery *was* solved and we knew what had to be done, getting the chef on board was a completely different exercise, or rather, obstacle. The story playing in the chef's head—"This skate wing costs $7.99 per pound, and I only serve an eight-ounce portion, so that dish costs me $4 and I am charging $21, which makes it a 20% food cost"—was not the complete picture and therefore inaccurate.

While a skate wing might be *delivered* at $7.99 per pound, it still needed to be cleaned, prepped, and fileted. By the time that was done, the price per portion could go up to $5 or $6. Not to mention the other items on the plate being served with the skate wing. Add crispy fried scallions, truffle-whipped yucca, sautéed fiddleheads, and we were up to perhaps $7 or $8 for the skate wing dish. And what about the skate wing that burned in the pan and had to be replaced with another one? Also, we needed to factor in complimentary bread service. At this restaurant, the chef liked to serve focaccia with an imported olive oil. We estimated that each guest consumed about one-and-a-half pieces of focaccia and about one tablespoon of imported olive oil, for an approximate cost of $.60 per guest. Now this skate wing dish had a cost of at least $7.60 and at the $21 menu price, that was a 36% food cost.

As is often the case, and was certainly the case with this chef, you can nickel-and-dime all day long about the "exact" cost of each component of this dish (maybe it's not exactly 36%, but we know for certain it's way more than 20%), but the bottom line remains the same: the chef is living in an "I'm at a 28% food cost!" world, and the numbers are telling us a completely different story.

Numbers don't lie. Follow the numbers, watch the story unfold, and adapt accordingly. That's what we are going to do in this chapter.

LET'S REGROUP

BEFORE WE BEGIN THE SURGERY on your business model and getting your finances back on track, let's review what we've learned so far.

- We know that Profit First is a cash management system built to instill permanent profitability in businesses.
- We know that MacDaddy PF Cash is the same Profit First model but built for the restaurant industry.
- We learned through Parkinson's Law *why* Profit First works—"we consume what we see"—and we learned about bank balance accounting, which is *how* it works.
- We completed your Instant Assessment (hopefully), discovering where the money is currently going in your restaurant (CAPs) and where it should be going (TAPs) based on industry standards.
- We also went over the logistics of MacDaddy PF Cash— how many bank accounts to open, what to call them, and how to use them.

- We reviewed what a business model is, why it's so important, and how to discover or rediscover your own unique business model.

So the question now is, how do you get from point A to point B? How do you move from your current situation, your current business model, to your business model at its best?

In other words, now that you know where the money is bleeding from via your Instant Assessment, or where your business model went off course, how do you stop the bleeding and get back on track? In the next two chapters, you will discover ways to decipher where you're making money and where you are losing it. Some of these tasks are simple, and I have created simple tools to help you with this process. Some are so simple and obvious that you may wonder why you hadn't thought of them first. I can tell you why: because you're thinking about too many things too often and without much, if any, intention behind where you spend your time and energy. You are so caught up in putting out those chronic fires, both real and imaginary, that the real "fire," the fire that causes your money to go up in smoke, isn't getting the attention it deserves. That ends right now.

In the "Menu Costing" section below, we will dive into the importance of pricing your menu accurately, and I will walk you through an easy exercise and downloadable tool to help you dissect what is happening with your food and beverage costs.

In the "Payroll and Scheduling" section, we will discuss ways to make the most of the labor and skill sets you already have on staff, and a tool for scheduling that helps to maximize efficiencies.

MENU COSTING

LET'S START BY GOING BACK to your business model or original projections and see how they differ from what is really going on. For example, if the projections in your original business plan showed your COGS at 30% but you're actually running 32%, well, that's a loss of $10,000 to your real revenue. Eye-opening, right? Not everyone associates 2% with a $10,000 loss, but in our example, that's exactly what this is. Let's fix it.

First off, let's all agree that this does not have to be an exact science, so please don't get hung up on the minutiae. We just want to get as close as possible to the actual cost of a menu item and, at minimum, have some number to use in determining what each menu item is truly costing you. What I sometimes find when working with restaurateurs, and just some people in general, is that if they can't come up with an exact figure, they just stop. They don't follow through, and they don't figure it out. But by doing this, what they are saying (or thinking) is that nothing is better than something. And when it comes to menu costing, among other areas, that is simply not the case. Here, something is absolutely better than nothing. "Nothing" would assume that you get all your products for free and the items you sell have no cost. When we put *something* in, we at least have something to work with. And remember, done is better than "perfect." Let's get this done.

Examine your menu pricing. I would start by choosing a couple of your most popular items in each category: food, liquor, wine, and beer. If you have high non-alcoholic beverage sales, look at that too. Once you choose these top sellers, dissect each down to its parts. For example, if one of your top sellers is a cheeseburger and fries, then list each ingredient, the measure of that ingredient, and whatever else you include on that plate, like tissue paper, a doily, ketchup, etc. Your list might look something like this:

MENU COST CALCULATOR						
					Menu Price	
Item:	Cheeseburger and Fries				$	12.00
		Unit Measure		**Price per Unit**	**Cost per Unit**	
Ingr:	Ground Chuck	8	oz	$ 0.41	$	3.28
	Burger Roll - Brioche	1	ea	$ 0.58	$	0.58
	Cheddar Cheese	2	oz	$ 0.21	$	0.42
	Lettuce	2	oz	$ 0.20	$	0.40
	Mayo	2	oz	$ 0.12	$	0.24
	Butter to grill Roll	0.5	oz	$ 0.10	$	0.05
	French Fries - Froz	5	oz	$ 0.25	$	1.25
	Ketchup in cup	3	oz	$ 0.12	$	0.36
	Pickle	2	oz	$ 0.15	$	0.30
				Total Ingredients:	$	6.88
				Menu Cost %		57%

Holy cow! That's a 57% food cost! On your biggest-selling item! And you thought you were running 30%!? I mean, if most of your other items have a very low food cost, then maybe they can offset this astronomical one. Let's pick another top seller.

MENU COST CALCULATOR					
					Menu Price
Item:	Nachos				$ 14.00
		Unit Measure		**Price per Unit**	**Cost per Unit**
Ingr:	Tortilla Chips	12	oz	$ 0.14	$ 1.68
	Ground Beef	4	oz	$ 0.41	$ 1.64
	Beans	3	oz	$ 0.16	$ 0.48
	Cheddar Cheese	3	oz	$ 0.21	$ 0.63
	Lettuce	2	oz	$ 0.20	$ 0.40
	Olives	1	oz	$ 0.16	$ 0.16
	Jalapenos	0.5	oz	$ 0.15	$ 0.08
	Sour Cream	1	oz	$ 0.10	$ 0.10
	Salsa	1	oz	$ 0.12	$ 0.12
	Guacamole	1	oz	$ 0.16	0.16
				Total Ingredients:	$ 5.45
				Menu Cost %	**39%**

Uh-oh. This isn't good. But maybe the drinks are carrying you. Let's dig in to one of those…

MENU COST CALCULATOR					
					Menu Price
Item:	Mojito				$ 10.00
		Unit Measure		**Price per Unit**	**Cost per Unit**
Ingr:	White Rum	3	oz	$ 0.70	$ 2.10
	Mint	1	oz	$ 0.10	$ 0.10
	Lime Wedge	0.15	ea	$ 0.33	$ 0.05
	Simple Syrup	2	oz	$ 0.10	$ 0.20
	Sprite	1	oz	$ 0.12	$ 0.12
				Total Ingredients:	$ 2.57
				Menu Cost %	**26%**

Okay, better. So, if you're selling a boatload of mojitos, they are definitely helping your overall COGS. But wouldn't it be better to control your food cost *and* have a kick-ass liquor cost?

We have created a tool for you to download so that you can menu cost items from your restaurant in a simple format like the one above. Go to www.profitfirst4restaurants.com and click on "Tools" to download the Menu Cost Calculator.

While you can do this for every item on your menu, that may not be necessary *right now*. This is where we pick our battles to first right the ship. Then we go back and tighten up everything else. Remember, our Instant Assessment showed us we only need to shave 2% off our COGS. We may be able to do just that by identifying a couple of our top sellers and doing one or all the following:

- Adjusting the pricing (usually the quickest way)
- Beating up vendors on price
- Creating a system for proper portioning
- And, if adjusting the price to anything even remotely reasonable still won't put that item in-line cost percentagewise, then you may need to get innovative by creating another top seller or popular item with a very low cost percentage that offsets the high one.

For example, maybe your bestselling, 24-ounce dry-aged prime ribeye costs $18 to purchase from your meat vendor. This is the best price you can get because you've shopped around.

And you know you can't charge $60 for it (to get a 30% food cost) because your customers would revolt, and you could get a bad reputation. However, it sells really well at the $49 price point, and you feel strongly about not going over $50 for any item on your menu because of the "optics." (Guest review: "Can you believe that place charges $50 for one steak? I'd better get the whole cow for that price!") In this case, it might make sense to leave the item alone and keep a lot of guests happy but create a side dish that goes perfectly with a dry-aged prime ribeye which, like all side dishes, is sold à la carte. Maybe it's a side dish of truffled linguine. You could serve it in a pasta bowl overflowing (for visual effect) with steaming, aromatic linguine, made for sharing or leftovers, for just $12. Let's see how that looks.

MENU COST CALCULATOR						
					Menu Price	
Item:	Side Truffled Linguine				$	12.00
		Unit Measure		Price per Unit	Cost per Unit	
Ingr:	Dried Linguine	4	oz	$ 0.20	$	0.80
	Truffle Butter	0.5	oz	$ 0.80	$	0.40
	EVOO	0.5	oz	$ 0.25	$	0.13
	Parsley	0.1	oz	$ 1.00	$	0.10
	Salt & Pepper	1	ea	$ 0.05	$	0.05
				Total Ingredients:	$	1.48
				Menu Cost %		12%

Heck yeah! No one can shake a stick at a 12% food cost. And given that this dish is both a visual delight and a tasty crowd-pleaser, and the guest is getting a great value because they can take home the leftovers for an easily heated, delicious lunch the next day, it's a no-brainer "hand-sell" for your waitstaff and bartenders. ("Hand-sell" means that all they have to do is mention it to guests using the description above and it will sell like hotcakes.)

Hopefully, you get the point that menu costing is important. And now you have an easy way to do it. Again, no need to do this for every item on your menu immediately. We're just looking for a quick win to conquer that 2% so we can move on to the bigger problem—lack of profit. But first, let's tackle payroll.

PAYROLL

IN OUR INSTANT ASSESSMENT, OUR payroll percentage is just one point (1%) higher than the industry average, or where we want to be. The solution to this could be something as easy as shaving thirty minutes off the start time of some of your hourly support staff (while maintaining your service standards) or letting some hourly support staff go home earlier on slower shifts. Here is an example of a labor schedule with hourly rates that fit what we entered on our Instant Assessment of $155,000 for payroll annually.

LABOR PAYROLL

FOH STAFF	# OF	START TIME	END TIME	TOTAL HRS	RATE$		
MONDAY	2	1	8	14	$6.00	$84	PER DAY
TUESDAY	2	1	8	14	$6.00	$84	PER DAY
WEDNESDAY	3	1	8	21	$6.00	$126	PER DAY
THURSDAY	3	1	8	21	$6.00	$126	PER DAY
FRIDAY	3	1	8	21	$6.00	$126	PER DAY
SATURDAY	3	1	7	18	$6.00	$108	PER DAY
SUNDAY	3	1	7	18	$6.00	$108	PER DAY
				127		**$762**	**PER WEEK**

KITCHEN	# OF	START TIME	END TIME	TOTAL HRS	RATE$		
MONDAY	2	1	9	16	$20.00	$320	PER DAY
TUESDAY	2	1	9	16	$20.00	$320	PER DAY
WEDNESDAY	2	1	9	16	$20.00	$320	PER DAY
THURSDAY	2	1	9	16	$20.00	$320	PER DAY
FRIDAY	2	1	9	16	$20.00	$320	PER DAY
SATURDAY	2	1	9	16	$20.00	$320	PER DAY
SUNDAY	2	1	9	16	$20.00	$320	PER DAY
				80		**$2,240**	**PER WEEK**

TOTAL HOURS	207
TOTAL WEEKLY PAYROLL	$3,002
WEEKS PER YEAR	52
ANNUAL PAYROLL	$156,104

GROSS REVENUE	$500,000
LABOR PAYROLL %	31%

Figure A.

(In this example, the FOH [front of house] staff hourly rate is $6 because their positions are tipped. Also, management would normally be included in this calculation; however, in this example, the owner is the only manager and is paid via the owner's pay allocation.)

The math works like this:

You scheduled your front of house staff to work a total of 127 hours per week at a minimum wage of $6 per hour (because these are tipped positions).

127 hours x $6 = $762 per week in front of house wages.

You scheduled your back of house (kitchen) staff to work a total of 80 hours per week at an average wage of $16 per hour.

80 hours x $16 = $2,240 per week in kitchen wages.

If you add your front of house wages of $762 per week to your kitchen wages of $2,240 per week, that gives you a total of $3,002 per week for payroll:

$762/week + $2,240/week = $3,002/week.

If you multiply $3,002 times 52 weeks in a year, you get $156,104:

$3,002 x 52 weeks = $156,104/year.

Give or take a few holidays and overtime, we're at about $155,000 per year in payroll. Again, this is 31% of your gross revenue of $500,000, which isn't terrible, but can we do better?

Let's tinker with the schedule and see where we might be able to save some time.

LABOR PAYROLL

FOH STAFF	# OF	START TIME	END TIME	TOTAL HRS	RATE$		
MONDAY	2	1	7	12	$6.00	$72	PER DAY
TUESDAY	2	1	7	12	$6.00	$72	PER DAY
WEDNESDAY	3	1	8	21	$6.00	$126	PER DAY
THURSDAY	3	1	8	21	$6.00	$126	PER DAY
FRIDAY	3	1	8	21	$6.00	$126	PER DAY
SATURDAY	3	1	7	18	$6.00	$108	PER DAY
SUNDAY	3	1	7	18	$6.00	$108	PER DAY
				123		$738	PER WEEK

KITCHEN	# OF	START TIME	END TIME	TOTAL HRS	RATE$		
MONDAY	2	1	8	14	$20.00	$280	PER DAY
TUESDAY	2	1	8	14	$20.00	$280	PER DAY
WEDNESDAY	2	1	9	16	$20.00	$320	PER DAY
THURSDAY	2	1	9	16	$20.00	$320	PER DAY
FRIDAY	2	1	9	16	$20.00	$320	PER DAY
SATURDAY	2	1	9	16	$20.00	$320	PER DAY
SUNDAY	2	1	8	14	$20.00	$280	PER DAY
				78		$2,120	PER WEEK

TOTAL HOURS	201
TOTAL WEEKLY PAYROLL	$2,858
WEEKS PER YEAR	52
ANNUAL PAYROLL	$148,616

GROSS REVENUE	$500,000
LABOR PAYROLL %	30%

Figure B.

Aha! We can! We were able to cut back just four hours per week on our FOH staff. (Figure A shows a total of 127 hours for FOH staff and Figure B shows a total of 123 hours.) That could mean eliminating just thirty minutes a day for one employee. And we only had to cut two hours a week for the kitchen staff. (Figure A shows a total of 80 hours for kitchen staff and Figure B shows a total of 78 hours.) That could be something as simple as letting cooks alternate who gets to go home thirty minutes early on four slower nights. Speaking in dollars, we just saved $7,488 per year on payroll.

Figure A. Annual Payroll, $156,104 – Figure B. Annual Payroll, $148,616 = $7,488 in annual savings.

That savings brought us to a 30% labor payroll, which is the industry average. Can we do better? Possibly. But we have bigger fish to fry. Let's move on to the real meat of the matter—achieving TAPs for profit, owner's pay, owner's taxes, and OPEX.

CHAPTER 9

This Is Where We Dial in Your Operating Expenses

As I mentioned earlier, when I switched careers from restaurateur to bookkeeper and consultant for restaurants and many other types of businesses, it was quite an eye-opening and unexpected experience.

My consulting firm grew quickly and before I knew it, I had a front row seat to the finances of more than a hundred businesses—many restaurants, but some retail businesses, salons, construction and design firms, law offices, realty firms, doctors' offices, you name it. I'm not sure there is an industry we have not serviced or reviewed.

But the biggest aha for me was learning that *all* these businesses had major challenges. Every one of them struggled or had a broken business model, and none of them knew how or why or what to do to fix it. Their owners knew something was wrong, that something wasn't working, but not one of them could figure it out. That's why we had work! That's why my business grew 2,600% in ten years. And we continue to grow and grow, year after year, because business owners need help. No one has it all figured out.

Sometimes even now when I see restaurants with lines out the door, full reservations weeks in advance, or running a forty-five-minute wait at 5:00 p.m. on a Tuesday, my initial reaction is, "They must be printing money!" But then reality sets in, I think of all the businesses I have worked with, and I remember that looks can be quite deceiving. Just because it looks like they're bringing in the dough doesn't mean that dough isn't flying right back out the door faster than it comes in. It doesn't mean that the owners aren't stressed out, overwhelmed, or unable to pay their bills.

All it means when you see a restaurant that appears to be successful is that they either have the sales side of the equation figured out or maybe the marketing and branding. Either is just one piece of a much bigger whole. And if a restaurant's business model is broken, all the sales, marketing, and branding in the world won't help; they could actually hurt. Money stays away from people who can't manage it.

I've watched business owners scrutinize every receipt, while I've seen others use their business bank accounts as personal piggy banks. I don't agree with either of these approaches. I don't think they help business owners or their business.

Business owners who labor over every single expense when it is not legitimately warranted are wasting valuable time. Time is money, but time is also energy. You need to harness this precious energy accordingly, especially given the long hours and days this industry demands.

I find that sometimes the business owners who nickel-and-dime every expense are control freaks. And I am okay with that if they aren't ignoring the areas that do need their attention.

If these owners are operating well-tuned business machines, sales are steadily flowing in, customers are ecstatic, costs are in line, and they are hitting their TAPs, then by all means, let them pick away at the little stuff if they think that's the best use of their time.

The problem arises when, for example, a business owner becomes fixated on a $9.99 CVS receipt they can't figure out while their payroll cost is ten points too high. They are choosing to obsess over this ten dollars because they don't want to face the much bigger problem going on in their business. Why? There are many reasons for this.

I think one of the biggest reasons is ego. And I don't necessarily mean ego in its arrogant form, but more of a prideful fragility. Business owners don't want to feel like failures, and running any cost that you know is too high may feel like failure. And then what if you're not sure how to fix it? That's another mark in the failure column. And what if you know how to fix it, but doing so will change the makeup of your business, affect your employees or your customers, and just be a generally difficult thing to do? Now you're a failure because you can't do what you *know* needs to be done.

Would you believe me if I told you that some business owners feel so strongly about not cutting certain expenses that their method of dealing with this is to not deal with it at all? They just keep doing what they're doing because they believe that all the expenses they've incurred are necessary, and it will all somehow magically work itself out, business model be damned. It is this philosophy that gets you into trouble and debt.

Running a business can be very emotional. I believe that running a restaurant can be an extremely emotional experience, more so than many other types of businesses. And because the restaurant industry is steeped in celebratory and emotional occasions, it makes sense that there are emotions flying all over the place.

Here's the thing: Your business model is not emotional. And at its most basic level, it's really quite simple. Your business needs to take in more money than it pays out. *You* get to decide how that looks, feels, and works because it's *your* model. Once you figure that out, once you have and understand a viable, profitable business model, then all you need to do is make it happen. This book will show you how to do that.

When it comes to looking at your expenses, you may need to "color within the lines" for a while to establish your working business model. This could mean trimming the excess and getting back to basics. Simplifying, managing, reviewing, understanding—all these tasks are based in strategy and creativity, not right and wrong or good and evil. No emotion. Just business. And more specifically, your business. Let's make it happen.

SOMETIMES THE MONEY IS HIDING IN PLAIN SIGHT

LET'S TAKE ANOTHER LOOK AT our CAPs and TAPs chart, especially "The Bleed" column.

		ACTUAL $	CAPs %	TAPs %	PF $	THE BLEED	THE FIX
Income Bucket	TOP LINE REVENUE/ GROSS SALES	$ 500,000	100%	100%	$ 500,000		
Bucket 1	COGS (FOOD, LIQ, BEV)	$ 160,000	32%	30%	$ 150,000	$ (10,000)	Decrease COGS
Bucket 2	PAYROLL (EXCL. OWNER)	$ 155,000	31%	30%	$ 150,000	$ (5,000)	Decrease Payroll
	REAL REVENUE	$ 185,000	37%	40%	$ 200,000	$ 15,000	Increased RR
Bucket 3	PROFIT	$ (9,250)	−5%	5%	$ 10,000	$ 19,250	Increase Profit
Bucket 4	OWNER'S PAY	$ 74,000	40%	50%	$ 100,000	$ 26,000	Increase Owner's Pay
Bucket 5	OWNER'S TAXES	$ —	0%	15%	$ 30,000	$ 30,000	Increase Owner's Taxes
Bucket 6	OPEX	$ 120,500	65%	30%	$ 60,000	$ (60,250)	Decrease OPEX

At first glance, shaving over $60,000 from annual OPEX may seem like a daunting task. It might feel impossible. To be honest, you may not be able to cut $60,000 in operational expenses. And that is okay. Don't worry about that specific amount. It's the goal, yes, but what's even more important than achieving that goal is the journey we take to try and get there.

We will start by taking baby steps, not giant leaps. That could mean canceling a subscription to an app, software, or maybe even a newspaper or magazine that you aren't fully utilizing. Or maybe you take a closer look at what you're spending on advertising and marketing, such as Google or Facebook ads, and dial that back for a while. Or maybe not every single Starbucks coffee or dinner out is a "business expense." The point is, there's a lot to look at and many places you can cut back. And while you may be thinking, *Okay, but that subscription only costs ten dollars a month* or *that Starbucks grande vanilla latte only costs six dollars*, all those little expenses add up, probably more than you realize, and small fixes can be enough to get the ball rolling.

One of the main reasons to do this expense analysis exercise is to get you in the habit of cost-cutting, of learning how to be frugal. It's like building muscle. If it's your first time at the gym, you don't pick up the fifty-pound dumbbells; you start small and work up. That's exactly what we are doing here. We want to get you thinking a little differently about where the money goes and how you spend it. These mini "cuts" can and do add up to a big impact on your finances and your restaurant as a whole.

Let me say this about frugality: I am not a fan. Or, rather, I wasn't a fan. I once thought that being frugal and being cheap were the same thing. And I don't like cheap anything. I especially don't like cheap people. But it's not the same thing at all. Another way to look at frugality is by answering the question, "Does my restaurant really need this, or do I just want it?" If you can get in the habit of asking yourself this question before every purchase you make for your restaurant, you will save a lot of money. And every dollar you save by not spending it on crap you don't need to deliver on your promise of an incredible dining experience is a dollar closer to profitability and a big step closer to owning a restaurant that thrives.

Now, there are always those people, I was one of them, who can make a pretty good argument for "needing" something that is more of a want. But when I realized that whatever I was contemplating purchasing was like adding weight to my restaurant when a business should be run lean and mean, I started to think long and hard before making a purchase and weighing my restaurant down.

We want our businesses, our restaurants, to be light and agile so that they can grow, thrive, and be profitable. So that they can weather any storm thrown at us. And we all know that storms can come from anywhere and in any form. When we weigh our restaurants down with a whole lot of expenses that they don't really need and maybe don't even belong to it (i.e., Starbucks runs, DoorDash for your kid's dinner, *all* Amazon purchases), then we aren't giving them a chance to become what they're capable of being.

If you are an athlete, or even just someone training to compete for an athletic event that you want to do well in, chances are you aren't going to go out partying for the weeks leading up to the event, gorge yourself on sugar and fast food, stay up late, not stretch, not work out, not stay hydrated, and still expect to do your best. The same mentality should apply to your restaurant. You cannot expect it to perform well, financially or otherwise, if you are weighing it down with a bunch of junk that doesn't belong to it. Maybe some of that junk belongs to you personally, and you may believe that you and your restaurant are one and the same, but please hear me now: you are not. And that mentality is what hurts so many businesses.

When I am meeting with a new or potential client for the first time, I often have to explain this to them (and hope they'll hear me). I especially enjoy speaking with owners of start-up restaurants and those becoming business owners for the first time, as I can usually drive this point home before it becomes a problem. And while lawyers and CPAs will tell you all about the ethics and unlawfulness of comingling business and personal finances, I don't come at it from that angle. While it is true that it is illegal to expense personal stuff through a business, and all sorts of terrible things can happen if you get caught, that's the least of your worries. Because if you run a business where comingling business and personal is commonplace, there is a good chance that your business won't be around long enough to really feel the pain of those choices.

EXPENSE ANALYSIS EXERCISE

REMEMBER BACK IN CHAPTER 5, when I had you look at certain financial reports to complete your Instant Assessment? One of those was your P&L detail report, which is a listing of all the actual expenses per category. For example, under "Advertising and Marketing" on your P&L detail report, you might find payments made to Google Ads, your social media companies, website expenses, etc. Under "Occupancy," you might see your rent payment, utility payments like gas, electricity, and internet, pest control, etc. This report contains all the nitty-gritty that makes up your big-picture P&L.

What I want you to do is print your P&L detail report and grab a highlighter. Or you can open this report in Excel on your computer and use the highlighter tool. That's fine, too. I don't use a lot of paper anymore, but for tasks like these, I like having paper in-hand and portable in case I prefer to do this exercise at home on the couch or while waiting in the pickup line at my kid's school.

In Chapter 5, we ran this report for one year, which is a great timeframe to use as it gives you the full picture of all your expenses. If your restaurant has been open for less than a year, then run this report for as long as it has been open. If you have yet to open your restaurant, this is a fantastic way to create a realistic, detailed set of projections.

In the following graphic, you will see a P&L detail report for one month. If I included a report for an entire year, that would take up too many pages and make it difficult to show you the exercise. This report lists the itemized operational expenses in each category.

PROFIT AND LOSS DETAIL REPORT Lucy's Bistro			
EXPENSES			
ADMINISTRATIVE EXPENSES			
Bank Charges and Fees			
	04/29/22	Bank Charges	0.00
		Total for Bank Charges and Fees $	0.00
Dues and Subscriptions			
	04/28/22	Spotify	9.99
	04/28/22	iTunes	9.99
	04/28/22	Inc. Magazine Online	20.02
		Total for Dues and Subscriptions $	40.00

Insurance				
	04/11/22	General Liability		100.00
	04/15/22	Liquor Liability		250.00
	04/15/22	Workers Comp		350.00
		Total for Insurance	$	**700.00**
Interest Paid				
	04/12/22	Interest Payment		67.50
		Total for Interest Paid	$	**67.50**
Legal and Professional Services				
	04/21/22	Bookkeeping		125.00
		Total for Legal and Professional Services	$	**125.00**
Merchant Account Fees				
	04/01/22	Ecard Systems		100.00
	04/04/22	CC Merchant Processing		500.00
		Total for Merchant Account Fees	$	**600.00**
Office Supplies and Software				
	04/01/22	Amazon		15.00
	04/02/22	Paper Supply Store		20.00
	04/25/22	7Shifts		20.00
		Total for Office Supplies and Software	$	**55.00**
Payroll Service Fee				
	04/08/22	Payroll Service Fee		25.00
	04/15/22	Payroll Service Fee		25.00
	04/22/22	Payroll Service Fee		25.00
	04/29/22	Payroll Service Fee		25.00
		Total for Payroll Service Fee	$	**100.00**
TOTAL FOR ADMINISTRATIVE EXPENSES		*($20,250/12 Months)*	*$*	*1,687.50*
ADVERTISING AND MARKETING				
	04/06/22	Help Wanted Ads		400.00
	04/06/22	Social Media Marketing		402.50
TOTAL FOR ADVERTISING AND MARKETING		*($10,000/12 Months)*	*$*	*802.50*

DIRECT OPERATING EXPENSE				
China, Dishes, Glasses, Silverware				
	04/05/22	Dishes & Glasses R US		300.00
	04/19/22	Dishes & Glasses R US		300.00
Total for China, Dishes, Glasses, Silverware			$	**600.00**
Cleaning				
	04/15/22	Cleaning Company		200.00
Total for Cleaning			$	**200.00**
Cleaning Supplies				
	04/04/22	Cleaning Supply Co		150.00
	04/18/22	Cleaning Supply Co		200.00
Total for Cleaning Supplies			$	**350.00**
Decorations				
	04/19/22	Flowers N Things		60.00
Total for Decorations			$	**60.00**
Laundry and Linens				
	04/05/22	Linen Service Inc.		130.00
	04/12/22	Linen Service Inc.		130.00
	04/19/22	Linen Service Inc.		130.00
	04/26/22	Linen Service Inc.		130.00
Total for Laundry and Linens			$	**520.00**
Paper and Disposables				
	04/01/22	ToGo Products Inc.		330.00
	04/08/22	ToGo Products Inc.		410.00
	04/15/22	ToGo Products Inc.		250.00
	04/25/22	Restaurant Depot		110.00
Total for Paper and Disposables			$	**1,100.00**
Restaurant Supplies				
	04/01/22	Restaurant Supply Co		105.00
	04/08/22	Restaurant Supply Co		105.00
	04/15/22	Restaurant Supply Co		105.00
	04/22/22	Restaurant Supply Co		105.00
	04/25/22	Restaurant Depot		80.00
Total for Restaurant Supplies			$	**500.00**
TOTAL FOR DIRECT OPERATING EXPENSE		*($40,000/12 Months)*	$	***3,330.00***

OCCUPANCY EXPENSE				
Property Tax				
	04/01/22	Property Tax Bill		200.00
		Total for Property Tax	$	**200.00**
Rent and Lease				
	04/01/22	LL, LLC		2,000.00
		Total for Rent and Lease	$	**2,000.00**
Repairs and Maintenance				
	04/02/22	Mr. Drain, Inc.		300.00
	04/11/22	Rest Equipmt Repair		600.00
		Total for Repairs and Maintenance	$	**900.00**
Pest Control				
	04/28/22	Pest Control		100.00
		Total for Pest Control	$	**100.00**
Utilities				
	04/09/22	Business Internet		150.00
	04/26/22	Electric Bill		250.00
	04/26/22	Gas		350.00
		Total for Utilities	$	**750.00**
Water and Sewer				
	04/01/22	Public Works Bill		250.00
		Total for Water and Sewer	$	**250.00**
TOTAL FOR OCCUPANCY EXPENSE		*($50,000/12 Months)*	$	**4,200.00**
TOTAL MONTHLY OPEX		($120,250/12 Months)	$	**10,020.00**

Now, using your eyes and your highlighter, review each itemized expense and determine if your restaurant absolutely needs that expense. If so, can the cost of that line item be lowered? Highlight each expense that you believe could possibly be lowered or eliminated.

Let's review, line by line, and see what we come up with.

Bank Charges are zero. Can't get much lower than that, and great job finding a bank that doesn't charge fees! Bravo.

Dues and Subscriptions are pretty low, but there is a twenty-dollar-per-month expense to *Inc.* magazine. While that's a great magazine, if you're not using it regularly as a benefit to your restaurant, it might be time to cancel the subscription. You can always bring it back later!

Insurance is an expense that should be reviewed every year. While you may have a great relationship with your insurance broker, the fact of the matter is that most brokers only work with a handful of insurance companies, and insurance companies change their "appetite" for different types of coverages all the time. For example, one year they may want to expand their restaurant portfolio and will offer competitive rates for restaurant policies like general and liquor liabilities. The next year, they may decide that they don't earn enough money from restaurants, so they increase their rates to offset the lower rates they provided the previous year. That is why it is important to shop around your insurance coverages annually to see if there is a better deal with another carrier. Though those rates seem fairly low in our example Instant Assessment, it can't hurt and won't cost you a dime to get another quote, so highlight that line item.

Interest Paid is a product of debt. This might represent interest on a loan, line of credit, or credit card. While this amount is relatively low for a monthly interest payment, you may want to investigate whether there is a lower-cost option available to you. Keep in mind that when you eliminate your debt, this line item will go away completely. We will be working on that in Chapter 10, but until that day comes, highlight this expense.

Legal and Professional Services are necessary expenses for every business. Even if you happen to be a lawyer, bookkeeper, accountant, CPA, financial planner, coach, etc. all rolled into one person, you will still want a second set of eyes on this important stuff. However, in our example, you already vetted other bookkeeping services before hiring this one and know it's the least expensive around yet still works, so you can leave this line item alone.

Merchant Account Fees are a necessary evil for any business that accepts credit cards as a form of payment. If you have been in the restaurant business for a while, you know that everyone and their mother claims to offer the lowest merchant processing rates. This is one of those things that solicitors love to hawk on the regular. And you must be careful who you sign up with, as there tend to be all kinds of hidden fees with many of these merchant processors. In my experience, though, if you find the right one and just monitor their monthly statements for any unusual fees, you won't have to worry too much about this expense. Generally, a merchant processor will cost anywhere from 2% to 4% of all processed transactions, but that number depends on volume, the types of cards people use at your establishment, etc. On this report, the merchant account fees are coming in at about 1.5% of gross monthly sales, which could mean either that Lucy's Bistro does about half their sales in cash or found a tremendous deal on their merchant processing cost. Either way, this line item is low enough that you don't want to change a thing. Just be sure to monitor this account monthly for any increase.

Office Supplies and Software is sometimes a place where business owners like to "hide" some personal purchases. That doesn't seem to be the case here, so we can move on to the next one.

Payroll Service Fee is another line-item expense that can start low and creep up without you realizing it. There are a couple of large national payroll companies that are known for just this tactic. They sell you on a super low payroll rate and only mention somewhere in the fine print that this rate is not locked in and can and will go up, sometimes quite high. Like the merchant processing fees, this line-item expense is one you'll want to monitor weekly or at least monthly. However, as with the professional fees, Lucy did her due diligence in researching payroll providers and knows that the rate she is getting is one of the lowest while also offering the service she desires. No work to be done here right now, but something to keep an eye on.

Advertising and Marketing is right on target, if not a little lower than the industry standard of 5% of gross sales. However, you want to be sure that you know your ROI (rate of return) on any advertising you purchase. Without a way to track that, you may as well throw money out the window. And yes, it is possible to track your advertising and marketing efforts. Therefore, while this line item is within budget, you may want to review these expenses to be sure you are getting the best bang for your buck. I would highlight this line item as something to circle back to after we find some bigger fish to fry.

China, Dishes, Glasses, and Silverware are all items you purchased when you first opened your restaurant. Or, if you are just getting ready to open your restaurant, these items are part of your start-up costs and not necessarily expensed. However, as time goes on and in the everyday hustle and bustle, dishes and glasses break, silverware gets thrown away accidentally, and you need to replenish. This is normal in our industry and that is why there is an expense category named for it. But this expense should be within reason.

If you find yourself purchasing glassware on a weekly basis, then you may want to look at how you are storing glasses. Are they falling from your shelves? Is the dishwasher too hot so they break in the machine? Is the brand of glassware you chose notorious for frequent breakage? Sometimes a simple adjustment like turning down the dishwasher temperature (while adhering to local health inspector guidelines) or storing the glasses a little differently (maybe one less row behind the bar) may help curb this expense. Lucy's Bistro spent $600 in one month on this line item and, while that amount isn't crazy high, there may be some opportunities here to shave money off this line item in the future months.

Cleaning Company and Cleaning Supplies are important and necessary expenses for most restaurants. A rate of $200 per month for the cleaning company—assuming that the work they provide isn't something that your current hourly staff could be doing before or after service—is a good one, and it may be hard to find a lower alternative. However, $350 for one month's worth of cleaning supplies does seem high. You may want to do a physical inventory of the cleaning supplies you now have on hand and determine how far you believe they should take you. Perhaps you feel you have enough to get you through the next two to three months; if this is the case, be sure not to place any additional orders or incur additional expenses. If you are correct, that could mean you just brought $350 to the bottom line for the next two months or so. But in order not to run out of anything, you'll want to get your management and ordering team on board and monitor the inventory weekly.

Laundry and Linens is also a common restaurant expense that can get out of control if not monitored regularly. At an expense of $130 per week, we can assume that Lucy's Bistro is only getting kitchen towels and maybe a couple of chef's jackets or pairs of pants. While this line item is relatively low, depending on what the linen company is providing, this area still needs to be managed and controlled. Without guidelines for usage in place, your staff could go through an entire week's delivery in two days.

In just about every restaurant I have worked in, kitchen towels and clean chef's jackets are like gold. And when you get down to your last few before the next delivery, they become more like rare blood diamonds. The good news here is that you can "Profit First" your use of these linens by simply allocating a specific number of them to each shift. Of course, according to Parkinson's Law, we make use of what we have. If you give a line cook twenty kitchen towels to use during a shift, they will use twenty kitchen towels. If you give them ten kitchen towels, they will make do with ten. So figure out an appropriate allocation per shift, communicate this with your staff, and lock the rest away. While it may seem annoying or contentious to have to police linens, this is basic restaurant management and needs to be done. Just have a system, communicate that system, and adhere to it.

The same is true for chef's jackets, shirts, and pants. Whether you decide to purchase them and require your staff to keep them clean and tidy, thus eliminating the laundry bill, or assign staff a weekly rental of their uniforms, create the system, communicate the system, and follow it. If you do this, you will know in advance what the cost will be each month. Without any systems in place, it's a free-for-all and this line item will most certainly increase.

Paper and Disposables is a line item that deserves attention, especially in this takeout-heavy culture that has developed over the last few years. And if your restaurant only does takeout or does it primarily, you feel this line item *hard*. You may even move this expense under COGS if the cost is part of every item you sell. In our Lucy's Bistro example, the first few weeks are averaging about $330 per week—all from the same vendor. And then it appears that during the last week, Lucy purchased her paper products from Restaurant Depot instead of her usual vendor with a savings of over 50%. With savings this significant, this line item is something you want to look at. If the savings were only 5%, or maybe even 10%, it might not be worth scrutinizing as there is an added expense associated with driving to Restaurant Depot, shopping and loading up your vehicle, and driving back to your restaurant and unloading the supplies or paying InstaCart or another delivery service to do this for you. But with this kind of savings, it absolutely makes sense to take another look at this category and find ways to improve it. Now that this line item has been highlighted, Lucy can determine a system that works best for the restaurant and experience some savings in this category.

Restaurant Supplies is yet another one of those expense categories that can get out of control if not regularly monitored. This category might include candles or votives, candy or mints at the host stand, check presenters, menu covers, table tents, crayons, and kids' menus—pretty much anything not already included in one of the line items above. Having a system for keeping this stuff clean, organized, and stored properly goes a long way toward keeping this cost in line. And as was the case with the "Paper and Disposables" line item, the regular vendor's delivery prices make these supply costs higher than Restaurant Depot's. Now an even stronger case can be made for moving your purchase of these items to a less expensive vendor.

Property Tax is an expense that comes as part of your lease or rental agreement. Not every restaurant has this expense, as it really depends on how your lease is written. If you have a "gross lease," that generally means that you pay a higher monthly rent, which includes many of the occupancy costs. If you signed a "triple net" lease, you generally pay a base rent plus all other occupancy expenses.

Prior to executing a lease, you should understand and agree to this expense. Then all you need to do is monitor it to ensure that it is in line with what you anticipated paying based on your understanding of your lease/rental agreement. Presumably, the only way to change this expense is to renegotiate your lease with your landlord. And since renegotiating your lease isn't something that happens every month, or even annually, this isn't necessarily a monthly expense analysis line item. However, when your lease is up for renewal, you should be well informed and equipped for those negotiations.

Rent or Lease expenses are usually among the highest expenses outside of prime costs. But just as I mentioned above, this expense is usually set in stone upon the signing of your lease and not a whole lot can be done to alter it until the lease is up for renewal.

Oftentimes, opening a restaurant for the first time can be very exciting. Sometimes there is a false sense of urgency about getting everything done—signed, sealed, and delivered—as fast as possible so that you can move that much closer to your opening day. And when you feel that kind of excitement and urgency, you may not always focus on advocating for the best deal for your business. This is a mistake. A lease or rental agreement is something that stays with you for a long time—for the life of the agreement—so it needs to be entered into thoughtfully, intentionally, and with eyes wide open as to how this will affect your financials.

Repairs and Maintenance is a necessary line item for every business, and for restaurants, it can be quite an active one. As I've said before, there are a lot of moving parts and pieces to every restaurant and shit breaks. A lot. Most of the time you can't just leave stuff broken, as you need it to run your business, so this is a sad but necessary category. However, what you *can* do is take care of the things you have so you can get the most out of them and keep repair and replacement costs down. For example, you can keep your equipment clean, avoid slamming your oven or refrigerator doors, and, most importantly, teach your staff to respect the restaurant and everything in it.

Lead by example here. Show them how you want the equipment treated and cleaned and do it with care and intention (which are contagious). Explain why that's important. While it may seem obvious to you because you're the one footing the bill, it may not be so obvious to your staff. And when a team member does a great job of keeping their station clean and organized, shower them with praise and ensure that the rest of the team sees and knows why you are making an example of them. This not only leads to a healthier, happier work environment, it also shines through in the service and the experience you provide for your guests.

Pest Control is another necessary evil for all restaurants. And there is no shortage of pest control companies, so do your due diligence to find one that is both reasonably priced and very good at what they do. That said, there is a direct correlation between the level of cleanliness in your restaurant and the level of pest control you need. Bottom line, a clean restaurant equals lower expenses.

Utilities for a restaurant can often be a larger expense item than you find in most other businesses of the same size. From the gas that is used for all the cooking equipment to the longer hours cooling or heating the building, utilities can run high. And good luck negotiating with a utility company for a lower rate. What you can do is set certain controls when it comes to the temperature of your restaurant rather than allow just anyone on staff to raise or lower it at their own discretion.

You may want to invest in a smart system like Nest that adjusts the temperature as needed or keep one manager in charge of it during each shift. Also—and I learned this the hard way with my restaurants—there are some preventative maintenance measures you can take with your utility equipment so that it functions longer and at its greatest capacity. For example, many heating and cooling units have a filter that must be replaced and/or cleaned regularly. When you don't do this, the filter can get clogged, thus restricting the airflow to the unit. This restricted air flow makes it work that much harder, which not only shortens the life of the unit, but also diminishes its functionality.

Many HVAC and equipment repair businesses offer preventative maintenance packages where they come into your restaurant quarterly or biannually to check on functionality, maybe clean or replace filters, and basically monitor and update you on the state of your equipment. They can also recommend daily or weekly maintenance that you and your team can perform to help prolong the life of your equipment and get the most out of it. Also, many states with eco-friendly initiatives offer programs where they send in an energy auditor to measure the amount of energy your restaurant is using and offer ways to reduce or conserve it. Bottom line, having systems in place and taking care of your utility equipment using preventative maintenance measures can go a long way toward keeping your utility and energy costs as low as possible.

Water and Sewer is often considered another utility and, much like your other utilities, attempting to negotiate a lower rate is usually futile. But what you can control, to a point, is usage. So be sure that your faucets don't leak and that toilets are functioning as they should. You may also want to look into high-efficiency dish- and glass-washers to conserve water use.

If your restaurant is on a property that is shared with other businesses, be sure that your utilities are metered separately and accurately. In other words, you want to make sure that you aren't paying for someone else's use of these utilities. This is something your landlord should provide proof of, and you'll want it confirmed prior to executing a lease. If you are looking to purchase the property, then ensuring that the utilities are metered properly is part of your due diligence. In the end, you don't have a whole lot of control over this line item once your restaurant is up and running other than your maintenance of the equipment, as with the last few line items.

EXPENSE ANALYSIS SUMMARY

NOW THAT WE'VE CONCLUDED OUR expense analysis exercise, here's our highlighted report of categories we can investigate for possible savings.

PROFIT AND LOSS DETAIL REPORT Lucy's Bistro			
EXPENSES			
ADMINISTRATIVE EXPENSES			
Bank Charges and Fees			
	04/29/22	Bank Charges	0.00
		Total for Bank Charges and Fees	$ 0.00
Dues and Subscriptions			
	04/28/22	Spotify	9.99
	04/28/22	iTunes	9.99
	04/28/22	Inc. Magazine Online	20.02
		Total for Dues and Subscriptions	$ 40.00
Insurance			
	04/11/22	General Liability	100.00
	04/15/22	Liquor Liability	250.00
	04/15/22	Workers Comp	350.00
		Total for Insurance	$ 700.00
Interest Paid			
	04/12/22	Interest Payment	67.50
		Total for Interest Paid	$ 67.50
Legal and Professional Services			
	04/21/22	Bookkeeping	125.00
		Total for Legal and Professional Services	$ 125.00
Merchant Account Fees			
	04/01/22	Ecard Systems	100.00

		CC Merchant	
	04/04/22	Processing	500.00
Total for Merchant Account Fees			$ 600.00

Office Supplies and Software

	04/01/22	Amazon	15.00
	04/02/22	Paper Supply Store	20.00
	04/25/22	7Shifts	20.00
Total for Office Supplies and Software			$ 55.00

Payroll Service Fee

	04/08/22	Payroll Service Fee	25.00
	04/15/22	Payroll Service Fee	25.00
	04/22/22	Payroll Service Fee	25.00
	04/29/22	Payroll Service Fee	25.00
Total for Payroll Service Fee			$ 100.00
TOTAL FOR ADMINISTRATIVE EXPENSES		*($20,250/12 Months)*	$ 1,687.50

ADVERTISING AND MARKETING

	04/06/22	Help Wanted Ads	400.00
	04/06/22	Social Media Marketing	402.50
TOTAL FOR ADVERTISING AND MARKETING		*($10,000/12 Months)*	$ 802.50

DIRECT OPERATING EXPENSE

China, Dishes, Glasses, Silverware

	04/05/22	Dishes & Glasses R US	300.00
	04/19/22	Dishes & Glasses R US	300.00
Total for China, Dishes, Glasses, Silverware			$ 600.00

Cleaning

	04/15/22	Cleaning Company	200.00
Total for Cleaning			$ 200.00

Cleaning Supplies

	04/04/22	Cleaning Supply Co	150.00
	04/18/22	Cleaning Supply Co	200.00
Total for Cleaning Supplies			$ 350.00

Decorations				
	04/19/22	Flowers N Things		60.00
		Total for Decorations	**$**	**60.00**
Laundry and Linens				
	04/05/22	Linen Service Inc.		130.00
	04/12/22	Linen Service Inc.		130.00
	04/19/22	Linen Service Inc.		130.00
	04/26/22	Linen Service Inc.		130.00
		Total for Laundry and Linens	**$**	**520.00**
Paper and Disposables				
	04/01/22	ToGo Products Inc.		330.00
	04/08/22	ToGo Products Inc.		410.00
	04/15/22	ToGo Products Inc.		250.00
	04/25/22	Restaurant Depot		110.00
		Total for Paper and Disposables	**$**	**1,100.00**
Restaurant Supplies				
	04/01/22	Restaurant Supply Co		105.00
	04/08/22	Restaurant Supply Co		105.00
	04/15/22	Restaurant Supply Co		105.00
	04/22/22	Restaurant Supply Co		105.00
	04/25/22	Restaurant Depot		80.00
		Total for Restaurant Supplies	**$**	**500.00**
TOTAL FOR DIRECT OPERATING EXPENSE		*($40,000/12 Months)*	**$**	***3,330.00***
OCCUPANCY EXPENSE				
Property Tax				
	04/01/22	Property Tax Bill		200.00
		Total for Property Tax	**$**	**200.00**
Rent and Lease				
	04/01/22	LL, LLC		2,000.00
		Total for Rent and Lease	**$**	**2,000.00**
Repairs and Maintenance				
	04/02/22	Mr. Drain, Inc.		300.00
	04/11/22	Rest Equipmt Repair		600.00
		Total for Repairs and Maintenance	**$**	**900.00**

Pest Control					
		04/28/22	Pest Control		100.00
			Total for Pest Control	$	**100.00**
Utilities					
		04/09/22	Business Internet		150.00
		04/26/22	Electric Bill		250.00
		04/26/22	Gas		350.00
			Total for Utilities	$	**750.00**
Water and Sewer					
		04/01/22	Public Works Bill		250.00
			Total for Water and Sewer	$	**250.00**
TOTAL FOR OCCUPANCY EXPENSE			*($50,000/12 Months)*	$	*4,200.00*
TOTAL MONTHLY OPEX			($120,250/12 Months)	$	**10,020.00**

To summarize even further, here is a list of possible savings and the monthly and annual total:

POSSIBLE MONTHLY SAVINGS Lucy's Bistro		
EXPENSES		**Savings $**
Dues and Subscriptions		
	Inc. Magazine Online	20.02
	Total for Dues and Subscriptions $	**20.02**
China, Dishes, Glasses, Silverware		
	Dishes & Glasses R US	0.00
	Dishes & Glasses R US	300.00
	Total for China, Dishes, Glasses, Silverware $	**300.00**
Cleaning Supplies		
	Cleaning Supply Co	150.00
	Cleaning Supply Co	0.00
	Total for Cleaning Supplies $	**150.00**
Laundry & Linens		
	Linen Service Inc	25.00

	Linen Service Inc	25.00
	Linen Service Inc	25.00
	Linen Service Inc	25.00
	Total for Laundry & Linens $	**100.00**
Paper & Disposables		
	ToGo Products Inc	50.00
	ToGo Products Inc	50.00
	ToGo Products Inc	50.00
	Restaurant Depot	50.00
	Total for Paper & Disposables $	**200.00**
Restaurant Supplies		
	Restaurant Supply Co	20.00
	Restaurant Supply Co	20.00
	Restaurant Supply Co	20.00
	Restaurant Supply Co	20.00
	Restaurant Depot	20.00
	Total for Restaurant Supplies $	**100.00**
Repairs & Maintenance		
	Mr. Drain, Inc	200.00
	Rest Equipmt Repair	100.00
	Total for Repairs & Maintenance $	**300.00**
Utilities		
	Business Internet	20.00
	Electric Bill	25.00
	Gas	50.00
	Total for Utilities $	**95.00**
Water & Sewer		
	Public Works Bill	25.00
	Total for Water & Sewer $	**25.00**
POSSIBLE MONTHLY SAVINGS		1,290.02
POSSIBLE ANNUAL SAVINGS	12 $	**15,480.24**

This annual savings of more than $15,000 covers the loss of $9,250 that we saw on Lucy's annual P&L, and that doesn't even include the savings we realize by reducing her COGS by a percentage point or two as discussed in the "Prime Costs" section in the last chapter. Therefore, if we take Lucy's Bistro's current P&L, adjust her COGS to 30% and payroll to 30%, and account for the savings we found in the expense analysis, Lucy's P&L might look like this:

LUCY'S BISTRO Profit and Loss	
After Expense Analysis	
	Total
Income	
Sales	
Food	275,000.00
Liquor	100,000.00
Wine	100,000.00
Beer	20,000.00
N/A Beverages	5,000.00
Total Sales	$ 500,000.00
Total Income	$ 500,000.00
Total Cost of Goods Sold and Labor/Prime Costs	
Cost of Goods Sold	
COGS – Food	85,000.00
COGS – Liquor	30,000.00
COGS – Wine	30,000.00
COGS – Beer	4,000.00
COGS – N/A Beverages	1,000.00
Total Cost of Goods Sold	$ 150,000.00

Payroll		
Kitchen Labor		52,500.00
Front of House Labor		22,500.00
Managers		75,000.00
Total Payroll	$	150,000.00
Total Cost of Goods Sold and Labor/Prime Costs	$	300,000.00
Gross Profit (RR)	$	200,000.00
Expenses		
Administrative Expenses		20,010.00
Advertising & Marketing		10,000.00
Direct Operating Expense		29,800.00
Occupancy Expense		45,000.00
Owners Pay & Personal Expenses		74,000.00
Total Expenses	$	178,810.00
Net Operating Income	$	21,190.00
Net Income	$	21,190.00

That's right: Lucy's Bistro is now producing a profit of $21,190 per year. That's going from a $9,250 *loss* to a potential $21,190 *profit* by making some slight adjustments to her prime costs and executing the expense analysis we just completed.

Is that the $60,000+ in savings that the Profit Assessment suggested we needed? Nope. But we did get as close as we could without sacrificing quality or service, we stopped the bleeding, and Lucy is now turning a profit. In a way, this new pro forma (which, in accounting jargon, means "financial statements forecasted for future periods") is now Lucy's baseline, the foundation for her financials, and a guide for the bistro's operation on a monthly and annual basis. This is the business model for Lucy's Bistro. And now she can build on it.

If her annual sales fall below $500,000, there is a little room in her bottom line to absorb that decrease, assuming all other costs stay in line or are lowered, without going into the red and losing money. This allows for some breathing room before the inevitable "Where's my Saturday night?!" panic ensues.

Now, if she experiences a significant increase in sales, some of her operational expenses may increase as well. But that's okay, because now that she has a baseline of expenses that Lucy's Bistro needs to operate, any increases should be in proportion to the increase in sales. She can monitor this by reviewing her monthly P&L as well as performing another Instant Assessment each quarter to find out where every dollar is going and where the bleeding is, if any.

The upside of doing the expense assessment is huge! Now that Lucy has implemented better systems, such as menu costing and thoughtful scheduling, as well as eliminated unnecessary expenses and controlled others, Lucy's Bistro is becoming a lean, mean, profit-making machine. Because of this, any increase in sales after prime costs will almost directly fall to the bottom line. For example, of the next $100 in sales, $60 will go to pay the prime costs (60%) but the remaining $40 will become profit or owner's pay or both, depending on the allocation percentages from the Instant Assessment.

This is how you build a profitable restaurant that runs like a dream.

PROFIT FIRST SUCCESS STORY

Caterer, Cape Cod

A YOUNG CHEF PURCHASED AN established catering company located on Cape Cod. I recall meeting with him in my office just before he finalized the deal in February of 2020. Talk about energy, this guy had it in spades. I remember him basically bouncing out of his chair, he was so excited to purchase this business and get ready for the upcoming summer season on Cape Cod.

When the COVID-19 pandemic hit in late March and shutdowns commenced shortly thereafter, he was one of the first people I thought of. I felt devastated for him. He had just invested a lot of money, time, and a boatload of exuberance and energy into this new venture that had abruptly come to a screeching halt. I reached out to him but didn't hear back for the rest of the year.

In comes 2021, and he's back with the same energy and enthusiasm, ready to hit the season running. By the spring of 2021, I think everyone was ready for a party and he clearly was not hurting for work. In addition, this chef had taken it upon himself to read *Profit First*, complete his Instant Assessment, open the appropriate bank accounts, and implement Profit First entirely on his own from the very beginning. He followed the instructions in the book step by step, and you know what? He *nailed* it.

His first full year in business, 2021, his gross sales were over $1.2 million. His food and beverage costs, COGS, ended up coming in at 44% (high) and his payroll was 19% (low); thus, combined, his prime costs were 63%. As discussed earlier in this book, the industry standard for prime costs for a restaurant is about 60%. However, as also mentioned earlier, the "right" prime cost percentage is based on your business model. Plus, this is a catering company and not a traditional restaurant, and therefore the business model is most likely a little different.

And there is also this—in the traditional Profit First model, which is what he used since this book was not out yet, there is just the one OPEX Account to pay all the business expenses including prime costs, payroll, etc. And while he did have a monthly bookkeeping service that provided him with his financial reports every month and his P&L did display high COGS at times, he did not necessarily feel it. This was partly because his labor was low but also because he was able to keep his operating costs low enough that he didn't experience a cash loss, meaning there was always enough money in his account to pay the bills. So rather than fret over high COGS, he chose to spend his energy on sales and delivering an amazing product to his customers. While his COGS were on the high side, his OPEX was on the money at 30% of real revenue, which translated into 70% of real revenue for his combined owner's pay, profit, and tax.

Putting dollars to those percentages, in year one he took home over $300,000 in profit and owner's pay. As someone who has worked with hundreds of start-ups, restaurants, caterers, food services, and other businesses over the last fifteen years, I can say with confidence that these results are pretty much unheard of. The difference between this catering company and all the other businesses? Profit First.

His second year in business, which is the year of this writing, he is on track to beat his first year's sales. He has been able to lower his COGS to 38%, keep his OPEX in line, pay his taxes, and continue to profit well into the six figures. How do his numbers keep getting better while he is also known as one of the best, most sought-after caterers on Cape Cod? MacDaddy PF Cash.

Caterer, Cape Cod	PF Year One	PF Year Two
Bank Balance	$240,730	$353,092
Accounts Payable	$25,758	$17,234
Net Income/Profit	$252,504	$340,927*

*Projected

CHAPTER 10

This Is Where We Get Straight on Debt

HERE'S THE THING ABOUT DEBT: it's not your friend. I learned this the hard way, as do so many others. As a young restaurateur, handling the money side of the business was pretty new to me. As a matter of fact, up until the last few years before I sold my restaurant, I don't think it ever really dawned on me that there was such a thing as cash flow or cash flow management beyond what I may have read in a textbook years prior, in college. I had always worked either in the kitchen, where no money is processed, or in the front of the house, where all I did was collect money from guests. From this perspective, all I saw was the money coming in. In the late 1990s when I worked at the Chart House, a fairly large corporation, all things money related were sent to headquarters (somewhere in California, I believe), where a team of bookkeepers and accountants handled the money for the restaurants under this corporate umbrella. As far as I was concerned at this point in my career, money was pretty much out of sight, out of mind.

My first restaurant job where I did handle both sides of the money—income and payables—was at La Bettola in Boston's South End. I mentioned this restaurant and its extremely talented chef in Chapter 8. La Bettola's lovely, gracious owners had a fairly loose grip on cash management. Maybe that's why they hired me even though I was twenty-five years old at the time and could barely pay my own bills. *But how hard could it be?* I thought. I mean, for years I had "collected" money (sales) for the various restaurants I worked in. How much harder could it be to write some checks and pay the bills?

As it turned out, it was extraordinarily difficult. It didn't seem to matter how much we charged for a piece of fish or chicken, or even how many we sold. We were constantly chasing our tails trying to pay the bills on time, or close to on time, or sort of close but not really on time. We had super busy nights and super slow nights; it was just like riding a wave, except there was never a destination in sight. Now that I think about it, managing cash flow might be a lot like navigating waves in the ocean. On a busy weekend, we might see land ahead! But as soon as Monday rolled around and all the bills got paid, we were back to treading water in the middle of the ocean with nothing but seagulls and miles of water in every direction… until Saturday night rolled around and we saw land again. Aaaaaand repeat.

Not long after I left La Bettola, I had the opportunity to open my own restaurant, Bomboa, with a couple of partners. I told you about this earlier in the book. But what I didn't tell you until now is that this is where I was introduced to debt. Not debt from the purchase of the restaurant, or start-up expenses; we were lucky enough to engage a group of investors who put up the money to get us started. This investment was just that, an investment. There was no specified time period during which we had to pay a certain amount, with interest, back to these investors. It was purely an investment, so they would be paid back out of profits.

LOL. None of us knew what profit was and as a matter of fact, I am not even sure the group of "successful" businessmen who invested in us really understood profit either. I would bet that they, like me and my partners, were living under the assumption that "Sales – Expenses = Profit" and that they would get their money back that way, via the leftovers. After all, the *only* way debt and investments are paid back is through profit. But since nobody seemed to know or understand what profit really was back then, or that it was a choice, I suppose we were all operating under the assumption that profit was a happy accident and we were just waiting for it to magically appear.

So not only were we responsible for paying the investors back through "profit," there was no timeline! Loosely speaking, the investors owned 95% of the restaurant (on paper, meaning that they had nothing to do with the operations or decision-making) and whenever we paid them their money back, they would own 40% of the restaurant in perpetuity. And that's how we opened Bomboa—with a bunch of money from a group of wealthy businessmen who had nothing to do with the operations of the restaurant and who would be repaid when we could repay them. I will add that we signed a very long, scary-looking operating agreement with these investors. I am sure it contained language that was much more specific and would have given them more control if we failed to pay them back. But they weren't looking to run a restaurant and my partners and I were very good operators, aside from the money management piece. We just didn't know what we didn't know.

Not too long after we opened Bomboa, cash began to run a little short. This could have been due to the fairly large salaries my business partners and I paid ourselves at the time—nothing crazy or over the top, but definitely decent. To this day, I don't know how we came up with the amount we paid ourselves, but I think it had something to do with what we felt we were worth. Or maybe we thought that was the going rate for rock star operators of awesome restaurants at the time. I can tell you for certain that it wasn't based on what the restaurant could actually afford to pay us.

Or maybe our cash shortfalls came from incurring expenses based on Saturday night sales—we had some pretty epic Saturday nights. Why not celebrate with a trip to New York City for a couple of nights, all expenses paid, to "research" other hot spots? We did. More than once. Looking back, after a big Saturday, we couldn't spend the money fast enough. I now believe we were under the impression that the slower nights simply paid for themselves, and a blockbuster Friday or Saturday was like winning the lottery. We sure spent money like lottery winners.

As it turned out, those slower weeknights did not pay for themselves, much less break even. Looking at an entire month a few weeks after the month was over, when the books were closed and the bookkeeper came in to review our financials with us, you couldn't tell that we had cash flow issues. The bottom line probably showed that we made a "profit" of a few thousand dollars—yay us.

We didn't know anything about profit then. We didn't know that it should be in a bank account named "Profit." We didn't know that it was a choice we could and should have made with every deposit. We didn't take it first, last, or really at all. We spent it before we had it or knew what it was, and therefore our P&L, in our minds, was just a report card. If the bottom line was positive, great! A+! We'd just keep doing what we were doing. If it was negative, we'd work harder on sales. Cutting expenses was not our focus because we were great operators! And our "profitable" reports proved it.

So when cash became an issue, when we didn't have enough to cover our bills or payroll, we did what we thought everyone else did; we borrowed it from anyone willing to lend it to us.

There are all sorts of ways to get money if you're a business with a constant stream of sales. There are traditional loans, and lines of credit that can be a little harder for many restaurants to get as the application process can be quite lengthy and thorough. Banks want to be certain that you can pay them back, meaning that they look for both historical profitability and projections of future profitability.

And then there are several unconventional ways to borrow money, which are almost always very expensive—so expensive that they can do more harm than good.

DANGEROUS DEBT

HERE'S THE THING—a P&L is not a cash flow statement, nor does it depict how the cash flows through your restaurant. And while it may show a profit at the end of a month, year, or any reporting period, that doesn't mean cash was never an issue. With Bomboa, we ran into many cash issues. And sometimes those issues wouldn't wait until the next Saturday night, or that next Saturday night wasn't quite robust enough to address the cash issues we had at that time. Enter debt.

Somewhere along the way, someone pretty smart figured out that businesses that take credit cards, especially businesses that are open every day or almost every day and have a large volume of credit card sales, are a safe bet for lending. I mean, if you're a lender and can attach your method of repayment to your debtor's credit card deposits, it could be a "win-win" situation. Or at least, you could market it that way. In the restaurant industry, this arrangement is commonly known as "merchant cash advance." And business owners who need the money, or think they need the money, will go for it. The problem is that these types of loans usually come with very high interest. But you don't necessarily feel the exorbitant interest because these lenders have made it so easy to not only get some quick funding, but also to pay it back. You don't really have to do anything but sign the original loan agreement. Somewhere in the fine print, it will (or should) lay out how much you have to pay back and have you agree to the lender attaching your daily credit card deposits until the loan is paid back in full. There's no sitting down and writing out a check to the lender every month, there's no automated debit coming from your checking account to make the monthly loan payment, and you rarely receive a statement (via mail or email) that breaks out principal and interest unless you specifically ask for it. Talk about out of sight, out of mind!

Because these lenders already know what kind of volume your credit card sales bring in (you will have provided them with several months of statements upon applying for the loan), they have already figured out when and how they're getting paid back. Some take as much as 40% of your daily credit card deposits until the loan and interest are paid in full. This allows the lender to be paid back quickly in the hopes that you will borrow again. "See how easy that was? How about some more money?" they might say to you. And because it was so easy, you may actually say yes without really thinking it through, thus digging your debt hole even deeper.

By the time these lenders are paid the money they loaned you plus the interest you agreed upon and possibly fees as well, you've paid them way more than you originally anticipated. If you borrow $5,000, you may end up paying them $10,000 in a short amount of time—at which point you completely lose control of your cash flow. The lender is now taking almost half of your credit card sales when your restaurant is used to, and should be, getting all your restaurant sales to use toward paying your vendors, payroll, meals tax, etc. Sure, you got $5,000 at the beginning, but if you borrowed $5,000 in this manner in the first place, you most likely needed it to pay something pretty quickly. If that's the case, that $5,000 is spent the minute it hits your account. It's gone. And now you're left with about half of your usual sales for the foreseeable future until you pay back your entire obligation.

This is dangerous debt.

WHEN YOU KNOW YOU NEED TO BORROW

"Okay, Kasey, I get it. But what am I supposed to do if I really need that cash to just get me through a tough spot?"

Good question. Here's how I go about coaching my clients through this.

1. **What happened?** This isn't an exercise in beating up my clients for any mistakes or mishandling of cash. This is strictly to figure out why the business is unable to pay its obligations. If the business model is working correctly, meaning it is breaking even or producing a profit, then there should be no problem paying the bills. And if you determine that the model *is* working, the question then becomes, "Where did the money go?" Most of the time, there are only two places to look beyond your P&L.

   a. The owner took it. This is very common. The owner might have paid themselves more than the business could afford, taken draws or distributions beyond what was available, or perhaps used it to fund another project. Regardless of what it was used for, the bottom line is that more money was taken out of the business than the business could handle, thus creating a cash shortfall.

   b. Debt took it. What I mean by this is that the only way to pay back debt is through profit. There really is no other way. And while debt payments do not show up on your P&L, you still need to account for them as they are most certainly a part of cash flow. For example, if your restaurant produces $5,000 of profit per month but you have $4,000 in monthly loan payments, then you have really only produced $1,000 in cash for that period. This is yet another reason why it's so important to understand what debt means to your business.

It's imperative to know what created your cash shortfall so you can fix it and not find yourself in this position over and over again. Good news! MacDaddy PF Cash will fix it for you. You will know exactly what to pay yourself, the owner, because you have a bank account with that exact amount in it—no more, no less. And since debt is paid with profit, which also has its own, funded bank account, you will have that money set aside as well. However, if your debt payments are higher than your profit allocations, you'll know you've got some work to do. We will get it done here, in this book.

2. **What do you need the loan for?** If it's for a vendor you've gotten behind on paying or even back taxes, you may be able to establish a direct payment plan with the vendor or government agency to pay back the arrears. That is more advantageous to you than taking out a loan. If it's for a piece of equipment, leasing options are usually available. If it's for growth, keep reading. If it's for working capital, meaning that your bank balance often hovers too close to zero and you need a cushion in your account so that you don't feel so stressed out, read on.

3. **What's your plan to pay it back?** Again: Debt is not your friend. That said, it is sometimes necessary. If your business is in growth mode and you want to expand in

some way, you may need to assume some debt to get there. Here are two examples of how to plan for debt.

a. Bigger loans. Let's say you want to add outdoor seating to your restaurant. After you've met with your city or town and discovered how many seats they will allow you to add, you can get to work on developing a plan to build this outdoor area. From these plans, you will get an idea of how much it will cost. Let's say that the city approved you for ten seats outside and you received a quote for $100,000 to build this out including patio furniture, lighting, heat lamps, all the bells and whistles. If you take the cost of $100,000 and divide it by the outcome of ten seats, you get $10,000. This buildout is going to cost you $10,000 per seat. Assuming you have to borrow the full $100,000, and since debt is only paid back by profit, each one of these new patio seats needs to sell $100,000 in food and beverages to produce the $10,000 in profit needed to pay back the loan (assuming a 10% profit margin). If the life of the loan is ten years, you could say you have ten years to generate those sales per seat, which means you need to sell $10,000 in food and beverages each year per seat. If you live in New England, like me, you know that patio weather can be fleeting; if you're lucky, there may be 100 days each year when the patio is open and people want to sit on it. That means you need to sell $100 in food and beverages to each seat, each year, for 100 days per year. With me so far? That's not $100 per table, that's $100 per seat. That means a two-top needs to spend $200. But that's for the entire day! So if you can turn that table twice each day, you only need to sell $50 per seat or $100 per two-top. If you can turn the table three times per day, that's $33.33 per seat or $67 per two-top. You get the point.

Other factors can help you weigh this decision about growth and incurring debt. Maybe installing this new patio will add curb appeal so that your restaurant gets busier year-round or receives more press, which could translate into more sales.

On the other hand, by going forward with this buildout and possibly having to add new exit doors or adjust the flow of your interior tables, you may end up losing some seats inside the restaurant to accommodate the new outdoor space. If that's the case, you'll need those outside seats to perform even better.

Or maybe you're looking to sell the restaurant in a few years and adding this outdoor space will bring more value. Then the question becomes, "Will the added value of this patio be more than what is left on the loan when you're ready to sell?" Meaning, is it worth it?

b. Small(er) loans. On a smaller scale, if you need to borrow money because you find yourself draining your account to near zero on a regular basis and you'd like a working capital cushion, you need to develop a daily or weekly plan to pay it back. Smaller loans tend to carry high interest rates, so the sooner you can pay them back, the better. Instead of going with one of those high-interest credit card attachment loans as described above, perhaps you open a separate savings account, nickname it "Loan Payback" or something similar, and then transfer 1% to 5% of each deposit to it and use that to pay the loan each month. Just remember that you needed this loan because you either weren't operating profitably or were spending all the profits in the first place. That's the bigger issue, and you want to be sure that you address it first.

Another example: Maybe you want to borrow money for a new app or website. Or maybe you want to invest in merchandise that you can sell. That may not be a bad idea, but make sure you have a plan for how this mini project will work and make you money.

If you're looking to create an app or revamp your website simply to make it look better, maybe update it so guests can easily make reservations or order takeout, these are really advertising and marketing expenses. And in such cases, rather than borrow the money, you should already have a budget in mind for your advertising and marketing spend each month. You may even want to open a bank account, nickname it "Advertising and Marketing," and begin allocating whatever budget percentage you determined would work for your restaurant to this account. Once there are enough funds in the account, it's time to get started. If you believe that you need to have the website up and running first, and that will help bring in sales or cut expenses, I would still set up the extra account, nickname it "Loan Payback" or "Advertising and Marketing," allocate the appropriate percentage, and use this account to pay the loan.

Here's the deal on debt… Believing that whatever you buy or invest in will "look cool" and maybe add some sales is one thing, but that thing itself will not repay the debt. Your *plan* will repay it. Without a plan, without a thoughtful strategy for using and repaying debt, you're just opening your business up to incur more dangerous debt. Dangerous debt is the debt you incur to pay for your existing debt or to cover up a broken business model. When you have that kind of debt, you know you're in trouble.

ANOTHER CAUTIONARY TALE

The Tavern

IN THE EARLY YEARS OF my consulting business, one of the restaurants I worked with was operated and co-owned by a friend of mine from back when I first started working in restaurants in Boston. Mike was a good operator. He understood restaurants and had worked in and managed them since he was a kid. He knew how to interview and hire, how to talk to employees, how to deal with chefs and vendors, and how to make guests feel happy and welcome. And while he may not fully agree with this, he, like many others, did not have a very firm grasp on the numbers.

I got to know Mike well over the years. And as of this writing, he is still a client today, operating two great restaurants. But back in the day, he had a certain way of looking at the numbers that I found baffling. I could understand where he was coming from in some ways, but to be honest, I found it concerning in most others. Here's why—his focus always seemed to be on treading water, on just getting through another week.

Mike was constantly treating the symptoms, putting Band-Aids on cash flow issues all over the place, but he never seemed to focus on fixing the problems that created those issues. That's not to say he didn't understand prime costs and expenses; he absolutely did, in theory. But I never saw him break a dish down to its smallest components and price it out like we did in Chapter 8. When we presented him with financials for the previous month and showed him a 38% food cost when he thought it was closer to 30%, he just assumed there was something wrong with our numbers and then spent time auditing our work to look for errors. This might be the part that baffled me the most. I mean, while we may not be perfect, the chances of us making an error that would cause food cost to jump eight points are very slim.

Part of our process in closing his books and presenting his financials was to reconcile, or balance, his accounts. If there was an error, we would not have been able to reconcile them and therefore would not have presented him with financials. Still, he would look for our supposed errors *all the time*. Not in a mean or accusatory way, he just automatically assumed that we must have made errors. And he was going to do us a favor by finding them.

Mike never found those errors, and all that time he spent looking for them could have been spent fixing the leaks. It was almost like he didn't want to see the truth. And while I am no therapist (though my team has been called "financial therapists" by clients and colleagues), I can think of a few reasons why this might have been the case. He may have felt that running a 38% food cost while assuming he was at 30% made him a "bad" operator. Or perhaps he didn't want to have to deal with telling the chef he needed to revamp the menu. Or maybe he was worried that he just wouldn't be able to fix the problem.

Mike's inability to accept that our numbers told the true story was the equivalent of sticking his head in the sand. He would spend valuable time searching for errors and when that exercise didn't produce any results, he'd simply move on to something else without ever fixing the problem. We'd see it again the following month, and the month after that. And why wouldn't we? Nothing was being done to stop the bleeding, and this restaurant was bleeding a *lot*.

The only reason The Tavern didn't bleed out earlier was that Mike kept using debt to patch up the wounds. I could be wrong, but I got the feeling that whenever he got approved for a new loan, he felt proud. He was the savior, and The Tavern could live to see another day because he was able to pay some bills... with debt. Oh, and did I mention that he also stopped paying meals tax for over a year? That's more debt. Remember those high-interest loans that attach their repayment to your credit card deposits? He went through *lots* of those and other terrible loans, not to mention money he borrowed from his family and friends.

At some point during Mike's career at The Tavern, he completely lost sight of the business model. The Tavern had been broken for some time and he just kept throwing good money after bad without ever stopping to fix the model. He didn't want to see it. His sole focus for years had been incurring debt while trying to sell the restaurant or bring on a partner. After close to two years of his search for a buyer or partner, I told him that the restaurant would never be able to pay back the debt it had incurred. It made much more business sense to shut down and cut his losses, maybe even file for bankruptcy.

Had MacDaddy PF Cash been around then, I think this story would have had a much different ending. Or no ending at all, as The Tavern could still be in existence today. My point in telling you this story isn't to show you how MacDaddy PF Cash would have saved the day—though it would have—but rather to illustrate the dangers of debt. Especially debt without a plan for repayment. Mike's "let's find a buyer" plan was really no plan at all, since he had no control over when that outcome would present itself. During the final months of The Tavern's life, the balance sheet showed over $750,000 in debt with no way to pay it back.

Debt is not your friend. You know that old saying, "Keep your friends close but your enemies closer"? I feel this way about debt. While it may not be your enemy, if you don't keep it in line, know what it's for, and control how it is repaid, it can take on a life of its own. And with predatory lenders making it so easy to borrow, it's not too hard to be swayed into thinking that debt is an easy way out.

You don't have to struggle to make it in the restaurant business. But you will struggle if you use debt to cover up problems that you either don't know are there or don't want to face. Having a working business model and implementing MacDaddy PF Cash will display your cash flow right out in the open and you'll know what to fix, immediately, to stop the bleeding. If you do need to borrow money, you will know exactly why. You'll also be able to create a plan to make it work for you and pay it back.

There is no shame in incurring debt. Almost every restaurant I work with has debt. Every restaurant that I worked *in* had debt. Sometimes debt is necessary. The major difference is in how you use it. How you plan for it. How you get rid of it. They don't teach you this stuff in school, in business classes, or even when you get your MBA, as far as I know. This is the stuff you learn the hard way, in the school of hard knocks. It took me a long time to graduate from that school, and I am sharing all the lessons I learned there in this book.

If you have debt, a little or a lot, that's cool. Welcome to the club. Now we know what it's all about and can kick it in the teeth.

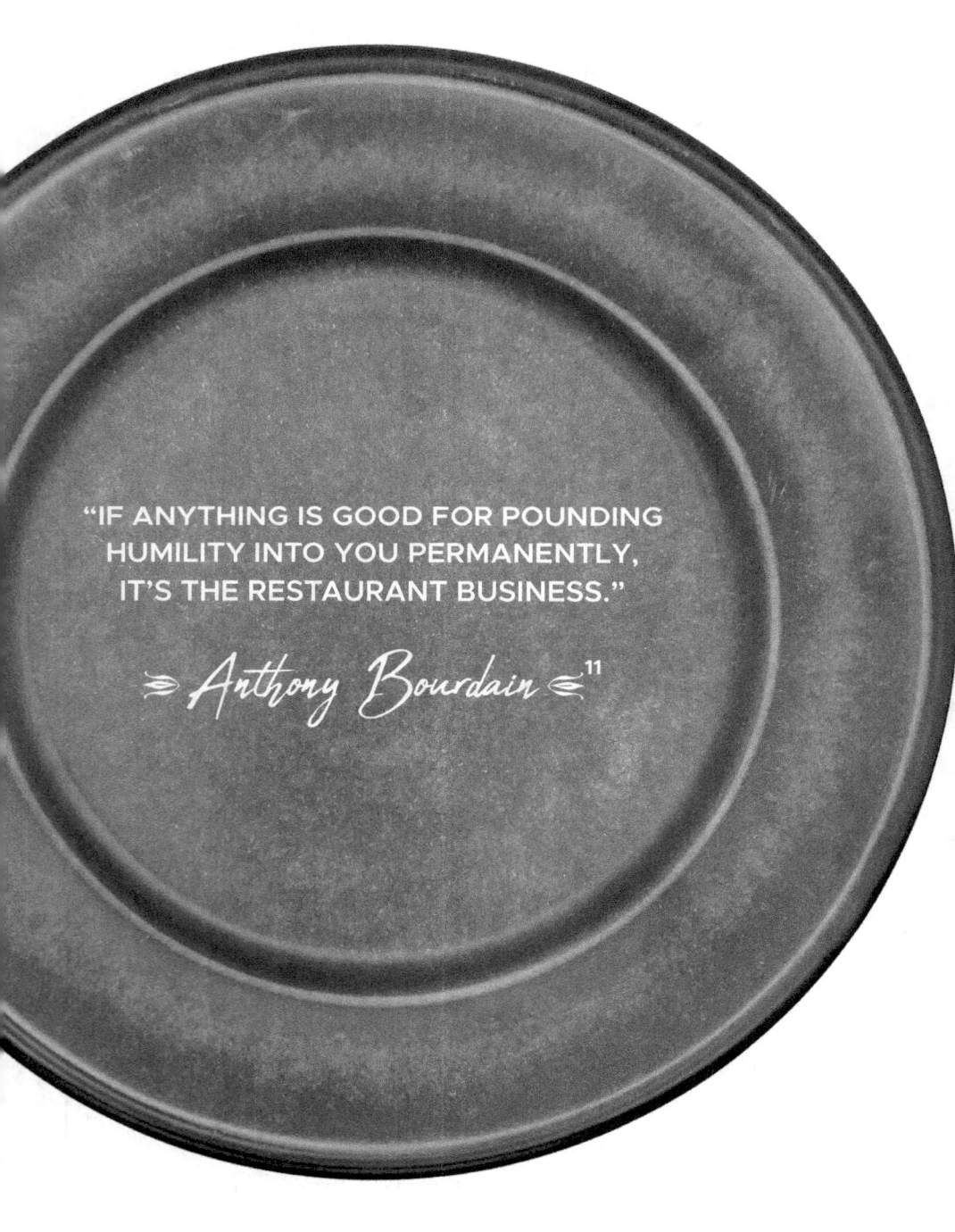

"IF ANYTHING IS GOOD FOR POUNDING
HUMILITY INTO YOU PERMANENTLY,
IT'S THE RESTAURANT BUSINESS."

Anthony Bourdain [11]

CHAPTER 11

This Is Where We Come to Terms with the Fact That Taxes Are a Thing

"A tax is a fine for doing well,
a fine is a tax for doing wrong."

—Mark Twain [12]

LISTEN, WE LIVE IN AMERICA. If you live in Canada or another country that imposes taxes, this pertains to you too. Taxes are not going away. Let's just accept that so we can all move forward and make some real money.

I say this because I am very aware of the myth/mindset that a "good" business owner should do everything possible to avoid paying taxes. I have seen all the tricks employed by business owners to attempt to mitigate their tax liability, and always backfires in one way or another. Put another way, wasting your energy trying to cheat on taxes is a futile exercise that reaps zero positive results, while the negative results can last a lifetime.

While I am not a CPA or an attorney, and I highly recommend that you speak with one or more about your business, I have been around this stuff enough to tell you what I know based on my experiences. But again, having a trusted CPA and attorney on your team is a must for any growing company. They can help guide you toward what is best for your business.

TAX LESSONS FROM A NON-TAX PERSON

Here's what I have learned over the years. As a business owner, there are a couple of different ways in which you may be subject to owing taxes. Your local and state tax liabilities will largely depend on the state you live in as well as the entity status you choose for your business: sole proprietorship, LLC, S-corporation, C-corporation, etc. Some of these entity statuses allow the business owner to be on payroll so that taxes are pulled from each paycheck, while others do not. Some statuses require the business owner to take "guaranteed payments" or "shareholder distributions," which are not considered expenses of the business and therefore do not lower the profit. And in most cases, profit is what is subject to taxation.

To get down to brass tacks, the government wants a cut of any money you make, whether that's through your paycheck as an employee, your profits and estimated tax payments as a business owner, or lottery winnings, capital gains, etc. The common denominator here is that someone made some money and the government wants their piece of the action. And if you think about it, how else would the government make money to do the things they do? If they left it up to donations, I am pretty sure we wouldn't have a government at all. So this is the system they came up with to run our schools, pave the roads, and fund emergency services and the zillion other things our tax money pays for.

Of course, that is an oversimplified definition of taxes, but it's good enough for us to understand what taxes mean to us, the business owners, for the purposes of this chapter. Your feelings about taxes—whether you agree or disagree with them, like them or hate them—have no bearing here. I just want us to agree that there is a tax system in place and, by law, we need to follow it. If you have strong feelings on this subject one way or another, they will not help you with this chapter.

As I have mentioned a few times throughout this book, I am very protective of how I spend my energy. Unfortunately, I am not one of those people who have an endless supply. I haven't met a lot of people over the age of eight who do. I recommend you use yours wisely. When it comes to taxes, you could choose to spend your energy fighting the system, lobbying, protesting, writing letters to your congresspeople, or maybe even running for Congress! Or you could just vote and spend your time and energy running a kick-ass business. Your choice.

Okay, so if we are all in agreement that taxes are a thing, let's move forward.

TAX MYTHS

IF YOU HAVEN'T BEEN REQUIRED to make estimated tax payments as a restaurant or business owner in the past, it could be for one of two reasons:

1. You continually run at a loss and therefore there is no taxable income.
2. Your tax preparer isn't helping you.

If item number one applies to you, well, those days are now over. Using MacDaddy PF Cash, we have just implemented profit in your business, which is a taxable event. *And that is a good thing.*

Let's dive into a couple of anti-tax myths.

Myth 1: The ole "Let's spend every cent we have before the end of the year so we look like a business that doesn't make any money." Hmmm. Okay, so, a couple of things wrong here. The first is, why would you want to look like you run a failing business? Just to get out of paying taxes? Here are all the things that can and most likely will go wrong if you choose to run your business this way.

   a. Running what appears to be a failing business could stunt your growth. You won't be able to get a business loan or a line of credit from a bank. Why would a bank loan money to a business that isn't profitable? After all, the only way to pay back a loan is with profit. So if there isn't any, how will this bank be repaid? They won't, because they aren't going to lend you a dime. This goes hand in hand with your business's lack of appeal to potential buyers. Even if you believe that you'll never sell, you should always operate in such a way that you are poised to sell—and for a lot of money. When this is your mindset, you will be sure to operate at a very high level, with maximum efficiencies, sales, and profit.

   b. The same is true if you are applying for a personal mortgage, a refinance, or any other kind of personal loan. Because you are a business owner, the bank will want to see your business finances. And evidence that you run a business that doesn't make any money is unappealing to any bank. How could you be a good credit risk if you can't run a successful business? At this point, I have seen some business owners try to plead their case: "Oh, those reports aren't accurate," they might say to an underwriter. "The restaurant makes plenty of money. I just spend it all so I don't have to pay taxes." Neither of these statements have helped anyone's case in obtaining financing of any kind.

c. Finally—and the easiest way to highlight how wrong this thinking is by putting it this way—what you are really saying by going on a shopping spree so it looks like you don't have any money is, "Let me go buy this thing for ten dollars so I can save three dollars." You didn't save three dollars. You lost ten dollars.

Myth 2: "Pushing income or expenses to the wrong tax years to lower your profit is a good thing." Businesses that file on a cash basis, which means they run reports and use financials based only on when activity hits their bank accounts rather than the dates on invoices and bills, will sometimes hold payments from customers that are received in early December, sometimes even in October or November, to keep their sales low for the remainder of the calendar year. These tax-procrastinators deposit all those payments in January of the following year.

This scheme is the definition of "passing the buck" from one year to the next, year after year—until when? Your final year in business? Maybe. But more likely, at some point you will want to show that you run a profitable business and won't be able to do so. Here are a few more problems with this game plan:

a. What about your customers who deliberately paid you in the current year so they can have real financial reports? If they too file on a cash basis, you just denied them an expense that they were counting on since they mailed you that payment five weeks before the end of the year. You could be screwing up their financials because you are deliberately trying to screw up your own. (Side note: This does not necessarily include deposits made or bills paid during *the last week* of the fiscal year. Once a check is mailed or hand-delivered, you no longer have control of the funds and, as a cash-basis taxpayer, you still can take that deduction.)

b. Doing this throws off your financial reports in a way that can be harmful to your business. First, it shows that January is a gangbuster month with all those deposits hitting your bank account when maybe January is one of your slowest months. And if you were to use these inaccurate reports to do any kind of projections or forecasting, they would be completely wrong because the software wouldn't know that you were trying to cheat the system. I suppose you could argue that because you are the architect of this hoax, you could alter your projections accordingly, but now we're opening a giant can of worms. I have seen this play out before. And it's very similar to keeping two sets of books for one business which, if you've ever watched any mobster movies, you know is completely illegal. You have your "real" set of books that goes to the accountant when it's time to file your taxes, and then you have another set of financials that you exported from the real set but adjusted to make real decisions for your business. Now you've got two sets of books for one business. Absolutely nothing good comes from that.

A former client of ours liked to do things this way. He would use the actual reports from the accounting software and then reshape them until they looked good (i.e., profitable) and submit them to a bank with his loan applications. What he didn't realize is that the bank would cross-check the reports he sent with his actual tax returns. Needless to say, they didn't line up. How do you think the rest of his application process went? Banks are not dumb. And he was not the first to try these shenanigans. If there were a blacklist among banks, this guy would be on it.

Myth 3: "I'll never get audited." Well, let's hope not. The entire point of an audit—a tax audit or any other kind—is to make sure that everything is correct. The definition of the word audit is "a formal examination of an organization's or individual's accounts or financial situation."[13] The state and federal governments know how to audit, and they certainly know what to look for when it comes to small businesses. It's one thing to maybe slip a couple of non-business meals on the books or maybe elaborate a tad on your home office expenses, neither of which I am suggesting you do, but those errors may just be "disallowed." In that case, the disallowed expenses are removed, which increases your income, which then increases your tax liability, and then penalties and interest are assessed on top of that. Not fun, but usually manageable. Hand slapped; now you will be more diligent about doing it right going forward. However, tax fraud, or "cooking the books," which is really what we are talking about in Myths 1 and 2, is an entirely different story.

When you look up "tax fraud" on the IRS website, the definition is broad yet clear:

25.1.1.3 (01-23-2014)[14]
Definition of Fraud

(1) **Fraud** is deception by misrepresentation of material facts, or silence when good faith requires expression, which results in material damage to one who relies on it and has the right to rely on it. Simply stated, it is obtaining something of value from someone else through deceit.

(2) Tax fraud is often defined as an intentional wrongdoing, on the part of a taxpayer, with the specific purpose of evading a tax known or believed to be owing. Tax fraud requires both:
- a tax due and owing; and
- fraudulent intent.

#notworthit

WHAT YOU NEED TO KNOW ABOUT TAXES

ENOUGH ABOUT THE UGLINESS OF taxes. Hopefully, you just learned that taxes are a thing and you have the privilege of paying them when you run a successful business. The trick is not to pay any more or any less than you should; that is where a good tax preparer comes in. If you don't have one, get one. Ask your colleagues and friends for referrals to someone who specializes in restaurant accounting and taxes. They may not be the cheapest, but they are one of the best investments you will make.

A good CPA or tax preparer will give you estimated quarterly payment vouchers with your annual tax return that tell you what and when to pay. The quarterly estimated payments are based on your previous year's tax liability plus 10%. That's the amount the government wants you to pay in each quarter. For example, if you owed $10,000 in federal taxes and $2,000 in state taxes last year, then you would be required to pay $11,000 the following year, or $2,750 per quarter, to the federal government (IRS) and $2,200, or $550 per quarter, to your state government (if you live in a state that collects income tax).

However, if your business is having a fantastic year compared to last year—and it will if you implement MacDaddy PF Cash—then you may far exceed the 10% increase that the government assumes when assigning your estimated quarterly tax amounts, meaning that you will owe more. And rather than wait until the end of the year to make a large payment, it may make more sense and be better for cash flow reasons to simply adjust your estimated quarterly payments for the last one or two quarters of the year. This is why it's always a good idea to check in with your CPA or tax preparer halfway through the year, and then again before you make your final quarterly payment, to see if an adjustment should be made.

If you are following the MacDaddy PF Cash allocations correctly, there should be enough money in your tax account to pay the appropriate taxes as your allocations are percentage-based. In other words, the more profit and owner's pay you have, the more taxes you will owe. And the great news is, once you get to your final tax return and the final amount owed for the year, any money left over in your tax account goes right into your pocket.

EXAMPLE: A RESTAURATEUR'S TAX LIABILITY

THE FIRST YEAR OR TWO of a business operation are often at a loss, and therefore incur no meaningful tax liability. There are usually a lot of expenses, training, and figuring things out in the first year that set businesses up to show a loss. Not uncommon. But say that a business owner wants this same scenario to play out every year. They enjoyed not paying taxes and, to be honest, they probably didn't have the money set aside to pay them if they did owe.

However, after the first year or two, as the dust starts to settle on the expenses and the focus is all on sales, this can create an atmosphere of "paper profit." And what I mean by "paper profit" is that the year-end P&L may show a profit, yet there is no such profit/money in the bank. This common scenario can happen for several reasons, but the most common is the owners' method of paying themselves. Because here's the thing: payments to the owners that are not run through payroll with taxes withheld (only S-corps and C-corps can have owners on payroll) are not allowed to be expensed and therefore do not show up anywhere on the P&L. And if the owner is working full-time in the business and taking a decent-sized salary in the form of draws or distributions (these could be checks written out to the owner, cash withdrawals, or transfers to the owner's personal accounts), this can and usually does create a taxable event even though there is no extra money on hand to pay the taxes.

To help illustrate this point, here is a collapsed P&L for a single-member, LLC-owned restaurant.

LUCY'S BISTRO Profit and Loss	
	Total
Income	
Total Sales	$ 500,000.00
Total Income	$ 500,000.00
Cost of Goods Sold and Labor/Prime Costs	
Total Cost of Goods Sold	$ 150,000.00
Total Payroll	$ 150,000.00
Total Cost of Goods Sold and Labor/Prime Costs	$ 300,000.00
Gross Profit (RR)	$ 200,000.00
Expenses	
Administrative Expenses	20,010.00
Advertising & Marketing	10,000.00
Direct Operating Expense	29,800.00
Occupancy Expense	45,000.00
Total Expenses	$ 104,810.00
Net Operating Income	$ 95,190.00
Net Income * Taxable amount	$ 95,190.00
Owners Pay & Personal Expenses	74,000.00
Actual "Cash" Profit	$ 21,190.00

In this example, the owner paid themselves $74,000 over the year. Thus, while the restaurant was able to generate a profit of $95,190, of that amount, the owner paid themselves $74,000.

So in theory, there is only $21,190 left over in real "cash" profit. And if this restaurant purchased any capitalized equipment throughout the year or had debt payments, those items do not show on the P&L either. Any piece of equipment over $500 is classified as an "asset" on the balance sheet, so you do not get to expense that purchase. What you do get to expense is the depreciation of that asset, which is an adjustment your CPA will make for you when preparing your taxes. And any payments you made toward debt would simply lower the debt or loan balances that are kept on your balance sheet. You do get to expense the interest portion on the debt, but not the debt payments themselves. (To keep things simple, I did not include depreciation or interest expense on this example.)

Using our example above, this single-member LLC owner, who paid themselves $74,000 over the year, also bought an oven for $5,000 and made a $1,000 debt payment toward a loan or line of credit each month. If I list those payments below, their "cash profit" might look something like this.

LUCY'S BISTRO Profit and Loss	
	Total
Income	
Sales	
Food	275,000.00
Liquor	100,000.00
Wine	100,000.00
Beer	20,000.00
N/A Beverages	5,000.00
Total Sales	$ 500,000.00
Total Income	$ 500,000.00

Cost of Goods Sold and Labor/Prime Costs		
Cost of Goods Sold		
COGS – Food		85,000.00
COGS – Liquor		30,000.00
COGS – Wine		30,000.00
COGS – Beer		4,000.00
COGS – N/A Beverages		1,000.00
Total Cost of Goods Sold	$	150,000.00
Payroll		
Kitchen Labor		52,500.00
Front of House Labor		22,500.00
Managers		75,000.00
Total Payroll	$	150,000.00
Total Cost of Goods Sold and Labor/Prime Costs	$	300,000.00
Gross Profit (RR)	$	200,000.00
Expenses		
Administrative Expenses		20,010.00
Advertising & Marketing		10,000.00
Direct Operating Expense		29,800.00
Occupancy Expense		45,000.00
Total Expenses	$	104,810.00
Net Operating Income	$	95,190.00
Net Income* Taxable amount	$	95,190.00
Owners Pay & Personal Expenses		74,000.00
Oven Purchased		5,000.00
Debt Payments ($1000/mo)		12,000.00
Actual "Cash" Profit	$	4,190.00

In this scenario, the taxable amount is still $95,190. As mentioned earlier in this chapter, the amount you owe in taxes depends on your corporate entity status, the state you live in, and perhaps other personal tax matters that you have going on. (Another reason why you really want to have a great CPA on board.) Based on these factors, it is likely that the taxes owed by this business would fall somewhere between 25% and 40% of the "Net Income" on this P&L. That means the taxes owed would be between $23,797.50 and $38,076 for that year in business ($95,190 x 25% = $23,797.50, and $95,190 x 40% = $38,076.00).

But as you can see, the owner only had $4,190 left over in actual cash profit. Where would they come up with the rest of the money to pay their tax bill?

That's a great question, but the IRS doesn't care. It's not their problem. And more often than not, business owners don't have that kind of money in savings. So they either take out a personal loan to pay it, take out a loan for the business and use that to pay it, or enter into a payment plan with the IRS (or appropriate government agency).

As you might imagine, this common scenario often leaves a bad taste in the business owner's mouth regarding taxes. That large tax bill usually feels like it came out of nowhere because there is literally no money left in the accounts to pay it when it's due. And this experience usually ends up with the business owner doing one of two things:

1. Burying their head in the sand and pretending that taxes don't exist for as long as possible, or
2. Spending their energy finding ways to do everything possible to avoid being "profitable."

Both are no-win situations.

Business owners who fall under item number one usually find their way to a CPA within a couple of years with a folder full of mean-looking IRS notices. But by then, the damage is done and it's just a matter of making sure their taxes are filed and current and then paying the piper. The avoidance tactic never works and is extremely expensive. In the end, it would have been much cheaper to have filed and paid on time, even if through debt.

SUMMARY

TAXES ARE A THING. ANY kind of avoidance, negligence, or game-playing will cost you more than the taxes themselves.

You don't have to struggle to pay your taxes. Taxes are a sign of a healthy, profitable business.

- Implement MacDaddy PF Cash.
- Hit your prime costs.
- Take your profit.
- Pay yourself.
- Pay your taxes.
- Dial in your expenses.
- Repeat.
- And never worry about taxes again.

PROFIT FIRST SUCCESS STORY

A Franchise Story

IN 2016, AN EXTRAORDINARILY SMART, ambitious, corporate-minded new restaurateur decided to invest in a breakfast/brunch restaurant franchise that was just entering the restaurant scene on the East Coast. As many do when bitten by the hospitality bug, she left a cushy corporate job, cashed in a good portion of her 401(k), and bet the farm with a large SBA loan to get her franchise store off the ground.

As is often the case with start-up businesses, especially restaurants, the business lost money during the first couple of years. That does not mean the restaurant was failing; not at all. In fact, her very first year in business they grossed $1.175 million, and the next year they grossed $1.41 million. That's a 17% increase! In the first two years! Note that I wrote "grossed" and not "made" or "netted." While the sales can be celebrated, her bottom line was no cause for celebration... yet.

There are a lot of unknowns when starting any business, but in the restaurant world, you can often multiply those unknowns by ten. And if you put a dollar sign in front of those unknowns, you've got a big cash loss. As I explained in the cautionary tale in Chapter 5, a loss on your P&L is not just indicative of a bad report card, it is money out the window. And replacing that money, that loss, often requires debt. This restaurateur started her business with debt and now she was adding more debt to cover the losses. This is not uncommon. But she needed a plan.

In 2019, her third year in business, she decided to invest her focus and money in more catering sales. After all, the restaurants were up and running, and while they weren't profitable yet, she believed that the addition of more catering sales could turn things around. And she may have been right. By the end of 2019, her sales topped $1.61 million with a profit of $9,000! Woohoo!! It looked like she was headed in the right direction.

But then came 2020, when the floor dropped out of the entire restaurant and hospitality industry. We all know what happened. Forced closures, no indoor dining, then dining six feet apart (maybe), no large groups, major renovations and cleaning initiatives had to take shape for restaurants to resume any kind of service—the list goes on. However, during this time, the government stepped up in ways I had never experienced or expected and began making funds and capital available to keep many restaurants and hospitality businesses afloat.

This restaurateur took full advantage of what was available in the form of grants and loans to keep her restaurant going. She also looked for opportunities to rebuild once we got to the other side of this pandemic. As a matter of fact, she opened a second location in early 2021. And in April 2021, she discovered and began to implement Profit First.

Her Profit Assessment immediately brought to light her biggest barrier to profit, which was food cost. At this time, she took the initiative to forge deep into the entire corporate franchise organization's inventory and pricing systems, putting new corporate-wide policies in place to help all the franchises gain a better hold of their food cost and inventory systems and thus become more profitable.

But creating and implementing systems is only one piece of the puzzle. Having a team that continuously executes and improves on these systems is where meaningful change happens and where permanent profitability can exist. With this knowledge, she invested in her own growth, leadership skills, and professional development *as well as* her team's. The decision to invest in her team's personal and professional growth may be the investment that pays off with the biggest, longest lasting dividends.

During the time of this writing, we are still in the middle of the COVID-19 pandemic. Staffing, or the lack thereof, is a hot-button topic for all businesses, especially the hospitality industry. This restaurateur decided to go deep on building and solidifying her management team—and the rest of the team—as these people would be instrumental in implementing the new systems she had created and in driving this business forward.

When asked if there was any proof that investing in the team was paying off, she offered this: From 2019 through June of 2022, the restaurants lost money for various reasons (as stated above). But from July through December of 2022, the restaurants grossed $2.1 million and netted a profit of $12,000, and that was after paying five salaried managers, including a COO, and the owner on full salary per Profit First guidelines. With this leadership team in place, this business is now poised for massive growth and profitability.

While many factors contributed to the success of this business, allowing it to pull through an unprecedented time in our economic history when so many had no choice but to close their doors for good, there are two things she knows for sure.

The first is that implementing Profit First has been a game-changer. While she already knew how to read and understand financial statements thanks to her corporate background, making the necessary adjustments to improve them in a simple, succinct, and powerful way was a completely different story. Implementing the Profit First Cash Management System showed her the clearest and quickest path to make those improvements. Following the system made it happen.

The second thing she learned was, she could not have done it alone. If she hadn't created a leadership team, and an environment where her entire team knew the stakes and were committed to the success of the business, the outcome would have been very different. The access to new capital and other opportunities she made use of during this uncertain time would all have been wasted had there not been a united, dedicated team in place to make her vision a reality. It takes a village. She knew that and she invested in it.

While it is hard to put a price tag on culture, leadership, and personal and professional growth, know that there is one, and it's usually quite large.

There is no substitute for company culture. The effects of your company's culture permeate every aspect of your business, from the top line right on down to the bottom line, your profit.

I would be remiss if I wrote a book about profit without mentioning the significant impact your culture has on it, for better or worse.

So, let's talk about culture.

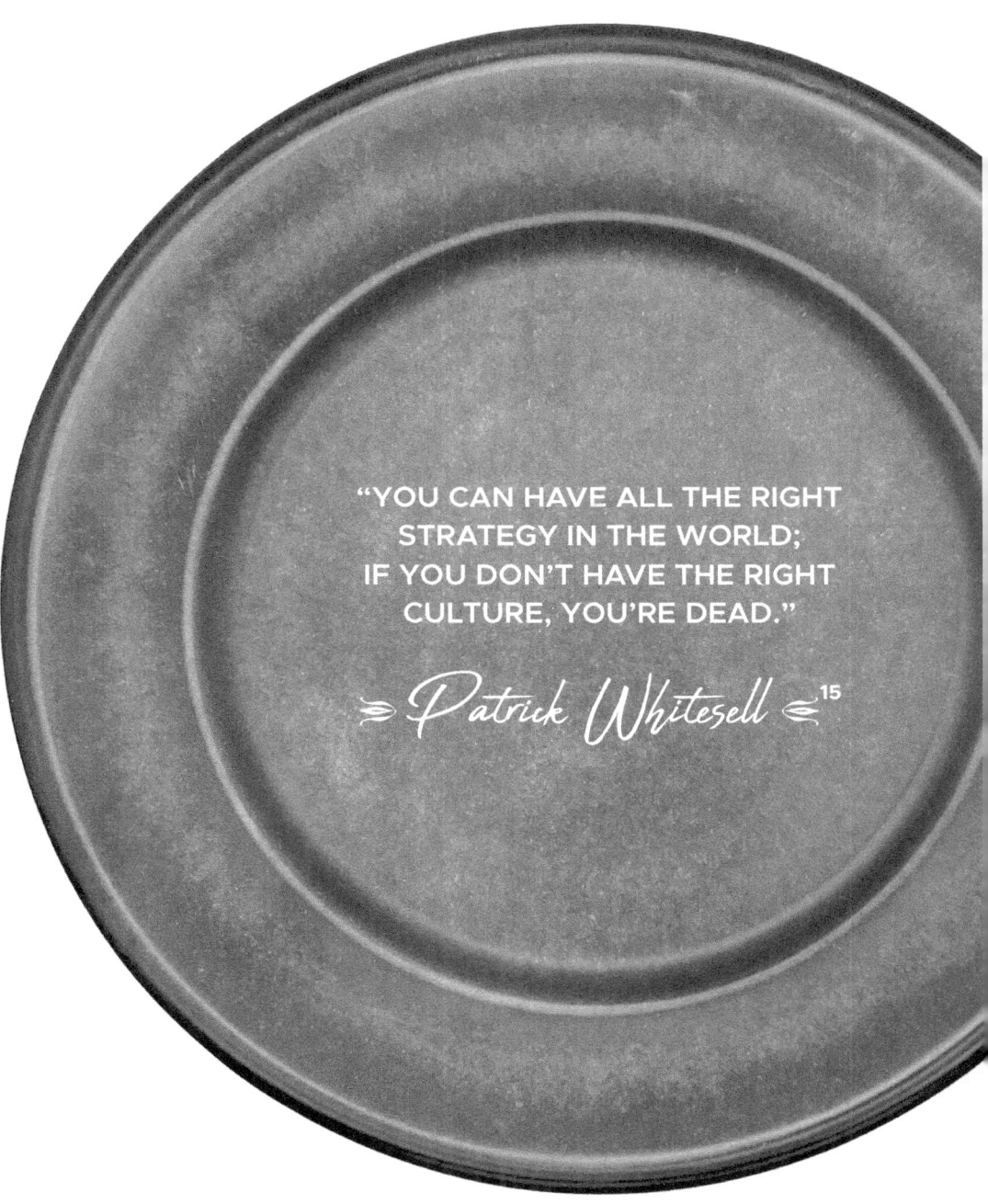

"YOU CAN HAVE ALL THE RIGHT
STRATEGY IN THE WORLD;
IF YOU DON'T HAVE THE RIGHT
CULTURE, YOU'RE DEAD."

Patrick Whitesell [15]

CHAPTER 12

This Is Where Culture Meets Your Bottom Line

FIVE GUYS BURGERS AND FRIES is a national chain of fast-food restaurants. It is your typical fast-food-style restaurant where you either order ahead and pick up or walk in, place your order at the register, and then move down the line to pick it up. Their menu is made up of burgers, fries, hot dogs, grilled cheese sandwiches, sodas, and shakes. Everything is served in brown paper bags. The restaurant decor is red, white, and potato sacks—very "wholesome American," some might say.

I have only visited the one located in my community, so I am not sure if they all have the same culture or not. But I have visited my local Five Guys many times over the years and the vibe, the culture, is always the same. It is pure, lighthearted fun *and* they clearly care about the product they serve and the experience they provide.

The kitchen is open, so most of the staff including the grill cooks, fry cooks, counter service people, etc., are on display. Sometimes there is singing amongst the staff. Other times it's playful banter, nothing offensive or over the top, and all in the name of getting it right. Moreover, every team member seems committed to your experience. They place your order accurately and with a smile and get it out to you hot and quickly, always with a few extra fries.

Again, I have not visited other locations, but if I had to guess, I would say that the extra scoop of fries they put in every bag is universal. And this gesture speaks volumes.

Five Guys serves all their burgers, dogs, and sandwiches in paper bags. Each burger, dog, and sandwich has a number sticker on it that correlates to the itemized receipt stapled to the outside of the bag. That way, you don't have to unwrap every burger to find out whose is whose. They do the work for you.

They then use a separate paper bag for the french fries, which come in different cups based on what size you order. They place the cups of french fries in paper bags and then throw in another large scoop of fries for good measure. And they do this with *every* bag.

Why? Why do you think they do this? I mean, at your typical fast-food restaurant, you get what you ordered. You ordered a cheeseburger and small fries? Then that's what you get, because that's what you paid for. (And you spend the rest of the meal stealing fries from your friend, who ordered a larger size.)

Five Guys is a big company. I have no doubt that they know about food costs, beverage costs, and all the other expenses we've talked about in this book. And I am certain that at some point there must have been at least one upper management person within the organization, whose job it was to watch the food cost, who may have said, "Hey, you know what? If we stop giving out that last extra scoop of fries, we could save (such and such) on our food cost!" And yet they continue to provide this extra scoop in every bag.

Mathematically speaking, if (for example) they could shave 1% off their food cost by eliminating this extra scoop, it could translate into a lot more profit, maybe $100,000 or more annually! And yet they don't make this change.

I don't work for Five Guys, but if I had to venture a guess, I would bet that they look at this extra scoop more as a marketing expense than an added food cost. It's something that sets them apart from their competitors. It shows that they care and want to provide value (even if in the form of extra calories). As a french fry-loving customer, I'm all about it.

But what I love even more about this approach is how it comes across in the employees in general. If you were the head fry cook at Five Guys, training a new employee, how would you explain this part of the training? After you trained on the fryolator, the oil, the temperature, and all the other things that create an amazing french fry, you would go over the cup sizes, the bags you use to place the cups in, and then the extra scoop on top —always, and in every bag. I suppose you don't have to say anything other than "Just do this," but even so, the act says something. It says that they provide more, not less, to their customers. They top off their fries. I think it's genius.

When you're out to breakfast or brunch and are drinking coffee, and the server comes around with a coffee pot, they might ask, "Would you like me to top that off?" Yes, please.

Or, if you ever watched the show *Cheers*, (I know, old, but set in Boston so I get to use it), the bartender, Sam (Ted Danson) sometimes topped off Norm's (George Wendt) draft beer as he sat on his barstool for hours at a time (something that probably doesn't happen as often today, but the sentiment is the same).

Merriam-Webster lists "top off" as a phrasal verb, which means "to end (something), usually in an exciting or impressive way." [16]

I don't know if many people have actively noticed or thought about the fry "top off" one gets at Five Guys. I know that it doesn't go *unnoticed* in that there has probably never been a complaint about not getting enough fries. And if you're the one serving up the fries and topping them off with that last scoop, you won't fail to notice that the sole purpose behind this task is to provide "more" for your guests—more fries, more value, more sharing, more smiles. So it is not surprising that this spirit permeates the staff, and thus the entire experience at Five Guys.

With one scoop, this company has ingrained hospitality into their culture.

If Five Guys were to run an Instant Assessment (as you did in Chapter 5), and it happened to come out that their food cost was too high, do you think their first course of action would be to eliminate that extra scoop of fries? Even though by doing so, they would alter a significant part of their business model and compromise their company culture? If they did, they could start to see a decline in their business that would be quite difficult to turn around. That extra scoop is what sets them apart not only in the value perceived by their customers, but also in the significance this holds within their company culture from the bottom up, or top down, or however you want to see it. The significance being that not everything begins and ends with how much money we can squeeze out of our customers or having the world's best food cost. Those things are important; we want to sell as much as we can to our customers and we want a great food cost—or one that aligns with our business model—but before those two things can happen, we need to connect to our audience, our customers, and show them what we're about and how we care. And both of those ideologies, value and culture, have a powerful and compelling effect on the bottom line.

Therefore, I believe that the extra scoop is already built into their business model and their food cost, and if their cost was running high, they would look for other ways to reduce it that would not undermine their culture. This is where culture and profitability intersect.

CULTURE IS CONTAGIOUS

THERE ARE A MILLION BOOKS about company culture. This is not one of them. But I am dedicating a chapter to this topic because it is crucially important to the experience you provide for your guests and staff, which has a direct link to your bottom line.

The culture of your restaurant is happening whether you are participating in it or not. In my experience, owners who do not participate in their company culture, whether that is *intentional* or not, often end up with the most toxic environments. And they usually don't discover this until it's too late and the damage is done.

It would be great if we could simply write up our mission statement and core values, show them to our employees, and then just assume that they will act accordingly, all the time. That doesn't happen in any business that I have ever heard of and especially not in a charged environment like a restaurant that involves a blend of all kinds of personalities. Someone with the temperament of a chef may not have the same temperament as a server or bartender, and vice versa. You may have heard the phrase "It takes a village," often in reference to child-rearing. I would offer that it also takes a village to run any restaurant. And this village needs all types of people. When you put a variety of different personalities together in a fast-paced, demanding, high-pressure environment, the results could be explosive, or they could be magical. The trick is to keep everyone on the same page, with the same goal of providing each and every guest with the best experience you can and *intend to* provide.

The most common way to do this is through the pre-service meeting or "huddle" that many restaurants implement before each shift. This meeting can be anywhere from ten minutes to an hour long and is the opportunity for the chef or manager to talk about the day's specials, menu items that might be 86'd (out of stock), the reservation count, any special groups or parties coming in, upcoming events, scheduling, staffing shortages, contests, etc. Some restaurants do this meeting during "family meal."

"Family meal" is the term used to describe the meal that the kitchen staff puts out for the whole staff, including themselves, before service. Generally, this is not food from off the menu, although it can be. More often, it's a giant pot of spaghetti, or soup, or some creative concoction that uses up the extra ingredients lying around the kitchen.

But family meal aside, this meeting isn't usually about the food. It's about connecting over a meal, getting clear (or as clear as one can be) about the night ahead, and getting on the same page with the same goal in mind, and, even more importantly, the same definition of winning. Winning in this scenario is achieving the best guest-focused experience you envision providing for your patrons.

It is so easy to skip over this part of the day, and yet it is possibly the most important piece. Getting everything ready and set up for service, whether in the dining room, behind the bar, or in the kitchen, takes a lot of work and involves many tasks. And a zillion different things can go wrong, or off-course, or get backed up or delayed, leaving a mad dash to get everything set up in time for the doors to open. Thus, no time to sit, chat, or eat. I get it.

But this huddle is where the magic happens. It's the calm before the storm, the human connection to what is about to happen in the service ahead. I believe that this pre-service meeting, this family meal, is sacred. And it can make all the difference not only in the service ahead, but also within your company culture. If you do not currently practice this ritual in your restaurant, I implore you to start. If this is not something you had planned to provide in your soon-to-be open restaurant, plan for it. Even if it means some staff need to come in a little earlier, or others need to work a little later to help set up for the next service, schedule it. This is a crucial part of your company culture.

While this gathering need not come across as a stuffy, Fortune 500 board meeting or a lecture by management, it should have some structure and an agenda. If you are consistent in your execution of this meeting prior to every shift, your staff will come to know what to expect. They will know how to participate and feel like they have a voice, and this will become part of your culture—a narrative led by you but inspired by your employees. This is how you get everyone on the same page. This is how you gear up for a busy, or maybe not so busy, shift. This is how you consistently provide your guests with *your* world class service.

Some people believe that within the nuclear family, the dinner table is the most sacred place. Studies have shown that the children of families who eat together are happier, healthier, and smarter.[17] Your employees are most likely not your children—at least, not all of them. But if you've ever managed people before, in any capacity, you probably know that it often feels that way. There are lessons to teach, boundaries to keep, praise and punishments to dole out, accountability to ensure, and, possibly one of the most important jobs—modeling of the behaviors you are looking for.

While you may not be the one to lead every pre-shift meeting, at least in the beginning, it is very important for you to set the tone. As the leader of your business, this is where you lead. To me, there is a vast difference between the "boss and employees" relationship versus the "leader and team players" relationship. I'm not going to go crazy with the sports analogies, though I agree that they are very relevant to establishing the culture you want for your restaurant. A coach is a coach, but a great coach is a leader. And by leader, I mean that you get everyone on board with your vision of how to execute the "perfect" service. This cannot be done by simply stating, "Do it this way because I said so," or by telling your staff to read an operations manual, or through their initial training, though that's a good start.

If you have ever worked in a restaurant, you know that it doesn't take much for things to quickly go off the rails. With all the different moving pieces in any given service, one wrong move—one oven goes down, one refrigerator stops working, one employee misses their shift, one glass breaks in the ice, one upset customer—and the whole shift can unravel. Shit happens, but it doesn't have to become a struggle. With the right mindset, you and your team can roll with the punches. After all, it's not hearts and lungs, it's dinner.

Unfortunately, keeping this Zen-like mindset is challenging. It can fade quickly and easily with the slightest annoyance. That is why it is imperative to make your pre-shift/pre-service huddle and family meal a daily event. Create it and allow it to be a time that everyone looks forward to and can count on.

We have created a sample "Huddle Agenda" for you to download to get you started. It is available with our other tools at www.profitfirst4restaurants.com; just click on "Tools." While we feel that it covers many of the basics you might want to touch on during any given pre-service, I encourage you to make it your own. This is your restaurant. Your culture. Your team. You know what inspires them and if you don't, find out. Ask them to participate and help mold your pre-service into a time they look forward to and actively engage in.

If you haven't already been having regular pre-service meetings, then you might meet with some resistance when implementing them with a staff that already has some independent, pre-service habits in place. Some team members might enjoy and plan on putting in their earbuds and jamming out to some tunes while polishing wine glasses, chopping vegetables, or slicing lemons, and have their part of the setup down to a science. Implementing this new "mandatory" pre-service meeting could throw a wrench into their setup mojo and they may not easily succumb to the idea. For this reason and others, I would make sure that, at least for the first several pre-service meetings, you have a very clear agenda, keep the meeting on track, and plan for them to last only about ten to twenty minutes. You're just dipping your staff's toes in the water. You will be giving them information, such as the specials and 86'd items, that they will appreciate when they don't have to hunt down the chef in the middle of service to get it. You can also use this platform to share any praise you may have for a team member, announce a contest, or even just ask what you can do to help make the shift run more smoothly.

For example, imagine if you learn that your guests always steal the servers' and bartenders' pens, and by mid-shift several of the staff must waste precious minutes locating a working pen so they can drop a check at a table that's been waiting to pay. With this knowledge gained from your pre-service meeting, you run down the street and buy a few packs of pens for a couple of dollars and load up the service stations and back bar with them. Not only did you just give a slew of lost minutes back to your staff, who no longer have to go in search of a writing implement in the middle of service; with this tiny gesture, you showed that you were listening and that you care. And if they model that behavior in turn, your guests will feel cared for as well.

Your company culture is a living, breathing character and very much a reflection of you. If you want that reflection to be its best, then that is who you need to be and show up as, every day, in a very intentional way. Easier said than done? Hell yeah. I'm sure Mickey Mouse has had some tough days like the rest of us, but we've never seen them. Imagine what would happen to Disney World if Mickey Mouse showed up pissed off or in a bad mood? The trick is to set up your company culture so that it becomes bigger than you and is being performed by your staff on a regular basis. On your good days, you get to super-charge that culture; on your bad days, maybe you step away and let your engaged staff take over. The key here, as with every other aspect of your restaurant, is consistency. You can consistently set the tone for how your culture shows up to your guests by having daily pre-service meetings that inform, connect, and invigorate your team.

We have all heard of crazed chefs and tyrannical managers. Maybe you've worked with a few. And maybe their restaurants saw some success, or had perceived success, but how many of those places are still in existence today? There is no longevity in toxic work environments. There is no stability in your team or the experience you provide to your guests, and thus no profits. And without profit, there is no restaurant.

Nobody decides to open a restaurant just to give themselves a job. People decide to open restaurants because they are building a dream. And whether you're a great cook who wants to share your love of food with the world or a great manager who wants to show and share your love of hospitality with the world, the common denominator is love and a passion for this industry that I have yet to see equaled in any other.

Now that you have dialed in your finances and are in control of your money with MacDaddy PF Cash, imagine: Every night of the week could be your Saturday, your Super Bowl! While sales may go up or down shift by shift, everything else could remain constant, including your excitement, joy, and love for this business. And *that* is contagious in the best possible way.

CHAPTER 13

This Is the Marketing Strategy That Saved My Restaurant

AND *NOW* WE CAN TALK about sales.

Now that we've dialed in your prime costs and operating expenses, implemented a system to manage the money, instilled consistent profitability in your restaurant, and talked about the importance of culture, you're ready for some sales strategy.

There is no way I could have started this book talking about sales and marketing. What would be the point if you didn't have a system for handling the money your sales and marketing brought in? What's the point of increasing sales when you don't have control over your costs? What if your business model is broken? With a business like that, more sales just cause more trouble. Sometimes, the last thing a business needs is more sales.

Take for example that cheeseburger and fries plate we menu-costed in Chapter 8. If that was your primary seller and you were under the assumption that you were running close to a 30% food cost when you were really running a 57% food cost, it would be a big problem, as we have previously diagnosed.

Perhaps you didn't realize your business model was broken because your bookkeeping wasn't accurate or you hadn't implemented MacDaddy PF Cash, or both. You knew that you were struggling, you just weren't exactly sure why; or you thought that struggle was ingrained in the industry, so you never really questioned it.

In our menu-costing example, every time you sold a plate of cheeseburger and fries, you lost money. And the more you sold, the more money you lost. Thus, trying to sell more of this cheeseburger and fries plate is just a bad idea.

There is no doubt in my mind that a restaurant owner in this situation would struggle to pay their bills, have debt, and think that the solution to all their problems was another Saturday of selling more burgers. And yet the reality for this restaurant would be that the more they sold, the worse off they would become financially. Remember Cassie's Burger Shack, the cautionary tale from earlier in this book about the broken business model and debt so deep that the only way out was to close? While not the same, the story is very similar. Again, if the business model is broken, the last thing you need is more sales. You either fix the model or close the doors.

But that's not you! You have been reading and following along. By now, you are beginning to see your restaurant through a new lens. It's not all about how many butts are in the seats every night. It's more about what you do with the butts you have. It's about controlling the cash, thus controlling your restaurant, rather than the other way around. It's about running lean, mean, and nimble. It's about systems, efficiencies, and giving every dollar a job.

If you build your restaurant model the way you envisioned it *and utilize MacDaddy PF Cash*, your business will fire on all cylinders, just like a car. Now that you've put your wheels into motion and begun to build confidence that your restaurant can not only run lean and mean, but also run better, it's time to turn the heat up on sales.

So let's kick this thing into gear, rev our engines, and feed the beast.

THE MARKETING STRATEGY THAT SAVED MY RESTAURANT

BEFORE I GET INTO THE brass tacks of how I employed this strategy at my restaurant, let's just unveil the naysaying, Debbie-Downer objections to doing this kind of direct marketing because believe me, I've heard a few. The two most common are:

1. "We barely make enough money now; how can we afford to give anything away for free?" and
2. "We'll look desperate."

I hope that as I tell you my story of how this played out for my restaurant, you will see how my strategy addressed both concerns.

As I mentioned earlier, our restaurant really began to struggle after September 11, 2001. While the industry started to bounce back months later, our restaurant also had to contend with other factors slowing down our sales. The biggest was probably the development of a nearby neighborhood that was becoming much sought-after real estate-wise. Developers were quickly buying up old brownstones in a neighborhood in Boston called the South End and turning them into gorgeous condos that sold for some of the highest prices around. Naturally, when you have a lot of wealthy people living in one area, some great retail businesses are sure to follow. And they did.

Several chef- and concept-driven restaurants, both established and up-and-coming, began to open among these remodeled brownstones. And because my restaurant was off the beaten path, located a few blocks away from the heart of this "new" neighborhood, it was hard to compete. We were good, but some of these new places were just as good if not better. They were the shiny new objects, the places to be seen, and they were closer to where many of our customers lived. Why walk a few extra blocks when you can just eat at one of five new restaurants that are all located within a block or two of your new condo? Our restaurant wasn't empty; we did have some loyal clientele. But it wasn't like it used to be, and those Saturday nights were very few and far between.

Also, our five-year lease was coming up. And while we had a five-year option to extend the lease, which we did, the rent basically doubled. Yup, you read that right. Doubled. You might be wondering, *How could you have signed a lease in which the rent doubles in five years?* Well, at the time we signed, five years prior, we just assumed that our sales would also double, or triple, or maybe even quadruple within five years. When we signed the lease, we simply believed that we were great operators with a great concept and lots of friends who liked to eat out, and if we built it, they would come.

It was as simple as that. And while I have definitely learned my lesson in the meantime, to this day I still encounter operators who believe that "if you build it, they will come." That is a dangerous way to think. It is really what your "best" projections might look like. Your lottery-winning projections. But you should also have projections for "if we build it, they will sometimes come" *and* projections for "if we build it, they won't come." Any one of those scenarios could play out, and you need to be aware of and have contingencies for each of them.

We believed in the "lottery winning" projections that were in our business plan, and we just assumed we would hit those numbers. We also had break-even projections and, as it turned out, we struggled to hit those. But after we received the investment and got Bomboa up and running, we never looked at our projections or business plan again. That was a mistake.

Because we didn't know about MacDaddy PF Cash at the time, we just assumed our problem was lack of sales. Thus, our sole focus was on how to bring in more money. I would wrack my brain thinking about how we could bring more people into the restaurant. One of my partners was a pretty popular guy whose large group of friends loved to go out several nights a week. They also loved to try new and trendy places. We would send him to those new places to schmooze with his friends and hopefully (somewhat nonchalantly) remind them of Bomboa and invite them to come back, as if they needed an invitation.

We also hired an expensive PR firm, briefly (because we couldn't afford it), and then tried to do what they did by creating and sending out press kits to promote new menus items or anything else we could think of. That didn't work.

We contacted every hotel concierge we could find to remind them that we were still there and awesome. That tactic met mixed reviews; some concierges were fans of Bomboa and, I believe, truly tried to send us business, while others were clearly not interested. Again, there were just bigger, flashier restaurants opening all around us and it was hard to compete.

Here's the thing that we did have: a decent-sized database of customers from our first few years in business who truly loved Bomboa. That list of people who already knew, liked, and trusted us had to be worth something, right? That list became my primary focus.

Here's what I did.

MARKETING THAT WORKS

WHILE WRITING HIS BOOK *GET Different: Marketing That Can't Be Ignored!*, Mike Michalowicz put out a request for stories of unique, tested and tried sales tactics.[18] When I saw Mike's request, it immediately brought me back to Rory Fatt.

When you Google his name now, you'll think Rory Fatt is kind of a big deal. He's a high-end business consultant, speaker, and author, and hobnobs with the rich and famous. When I first heard of Rory, it was in the early 2000s when he was running his company, Restaurant Marketing Solutions. I paid a lot of money—or a lot to me at the time—for a bunch of cassette tapes and several thick books that would teach me how to market my restaurant. These books contained hundreds of sample ads to use for any type of restaurant. The common theme among them was that they were *different*. Some were bizarre, such as "Order Thai Chicken in Your Underwear!" and "Entrepreneur Infuriates Restaurant Owners by Giving Away Free Dinners!" but what they all had in common was that they were unusual. They made you stop and think.

That is why Rory Fatt came buzzing back into my memory when I saw Mike's request. In my mind, Rory was the king of different. And I told this to Mike on a call after I responded to his post about unique marketing stories. As I began to tell Mike about my experience with Rory's company, I vividly recalled some of the marketing tactics I employed at Bomboa.

The one that stands out the most is the direct mail birthday marketing piece, which Mike ultimately included in *Get Different*.

DIRECT MARKETING THAT WORKS

It was about 2004 or 2005, and email was widely used. Because it was cheap or free, it seemed that all businesses were jumping on the email bandwagon. Snail-mailing anything was virtually unheard of. I mean, why would you pay to mail something when you could send an email for free? However, spam email was also at an all-time high, so what was once a great, extremely cheap way to market to your customers had become heavily diluted.

Rory Fatt explained that using snail mail was an opportunity because your marketing would not be competing with every-one else's. Everyone else was on email, vying for recipients' attention with catchy subject lines or colorful images. The old-fashioned mailbox had been abandoned by marketers and yet the recipient, the customer, still checked it every day, consciously or unconsciously hoping for something, anything, that wasn't a utility bill or an AARP mailing meant for a previous owner. This old-new marketing landscape was ripe for the taking. You could be the star of the show inside all those otherwise empty mailboxes! You could create some intrigue!

One of Rory's marketing tactics was to place a single birthday candle inside a plain white envelope with a letter you could easily print from your office printer that said, you guessed it, "Happy Birthday!" From there, the world was your oyster. You could personalize it by using their name, "Happy Birthday, Clyde!" or send them an offer: "Dessert Is on Us During Your Birthday Month!" Of course, there is always the common "BOGO" (buy one get one free) offer for an appetizer, entrée, or dessert. I mean, you could style this thing any way you wanted.

Why add the birthday candle? Because the feel of the mystery object inside the envelope creates enough interest to get the recipient to *open* the envelope. Without this bit of intrigue, they might presume you are sending them a generic advertisement with a copy of the menu or some other boring offer that they might easily toss aside. Plus, who doesn't smile at the sight of a birthday candle, especially when it's near your birthday? A small gesture can speak volumes. And it did for my restaurant.

Plus, now that they've received this paper letter, they have something to bring into the restaurant to claim whatever offer you put out there. You put a disclaimer, the small print, if you will, at the bottom of the letter asking them to bring in the birthday offer and give it to their server in order to obtain their birthday promo. This letter is how you track the success of this marketing strategy. And as a bonus for you, I've created a sample copy of this letter and other marketing tools for you to download. Go to www.profitfirst4restaurants.com and click on "Tools."

HERE'S HOW THE BIRTHDAY CANDLE MAILER WORKED

Do you know what a check presenter is? It's the small, usually black plastic tray or leather or vinyl folder in which you place the check before putting it down on the table. The folder or "book" model both hides the check and protects it from getting wet and has a pocket that you can stuff the check into, as well as a small pocket for a credit card to be placed in. This check presenter is a great piece of real estate and is often underused. Your guest must look at it, assuming they plan on paying, and it's usually the guest with the money. So now you've got a captive audience. This is a great place and a perfect time to tell them or ask them about anything. You could create a flyer insert that announces an upcoming event such as a wine tasting or beer dinner, or perhaps there's an upcoming holiday for which you will offer a special prix fixe menu. Basically, you can use this little check presenter book as a mini billboard for all kinds of announcements.

Another way to use this piece of real estate is to collect information and ask your guests about themselves—and who doesn't like to talk about themselves? Definitely ask them about their experience. At Bomboa, we created a "check presenter insert card" and placed several of them in every check presenter. That way, more than one guest at the table could fill them out. And we had our staff include multiple pens inside the check presenter so that the guests had time to fill them out before we ran the credit card or got them change. (There is a check presenter template waiting for you at www. profitfirst4restaurants.com; just click on "Tools.") Here is an example of what one might look like:

Guest Comment Card

To Our Guests: Please take a moment to complete this comment card.
We value your opinion and thank you for helping us to monitor the quality
of our products and service. If you add your name and address, you
will automatically be enrolled in our Birthday Club, as well as have the
opportunity to learn about other fun events and specials we're cookin' up.

	Poor				Excellent
SERVICE					
Friendliness	1	2	3	4	5
Timeliness	1	2	3	4	5
Knowledgeability	1	2	3	4	5
FOOD					
Quality	1	2	3	4	5
Appearance	1	2	3	4	5
Taste	1	2	3	4	5
SETTING					
Cleanliness	1	2	3	4	5
Comfort	1	2	3	4	5
Ambiance	1	2	3	4	5

What do you like best about our Restaurant? _____

How can we improve? _____

Was there anything you didn't like? _____

What items would you like to see added to our menu? _____

How did you hear about us? _____

Will you return? _____

How often do you eat at our Restaurant? _____

Name _____   Birthday _____

Address _____   Anniversary _____

City, State, Zip _____   Date _____

Phone _____   Location _____

A lot of great information can be gathered by using a comment card. More people are willing to give honest feedback on a form that they can leave behind than are willing to share it face to face with a manager or server. Whether this feedback is good or bad, *you want to know*. You need to know so that you can do more of the "good" stuff and less of the "bad." But the real gold mine in these forms is the data you collect: birthdays, anniversaries, favorite items, and mailing addresses.

While learning what you're doing well and what can be improved upon is important and can provide valuable topics to discuss at your management and pre-shift/pre-service meetings, we're going to focus on the marketing aspect in this chapter.

QUICK STAFF TRAINING

AT BOMBOA, WE HELD A separate training session with our servers and bartenders to discuss the importance of these comment cards. We also asked for feedback from our staff as they were on the front lines and spoke with our guests more than anyone else. They were able to provide valuable insight as to any edits we needed to make to our custom comment cards, and since we printed these in-house, we were able to edit them on the fly.

As part of their opening setup, we asked our service staff to place several copies in every check presenter, with extras on hand in every server station and behind the bar to make them quick and easy to refill. In addition, we purchased several dozen inexpensive pens at the dollar store so there would be plenty of pens for the servers to give out when dropping off the check presenters at the tables.

Next, we trained our staff on how to "sell" the use of these comment cards. Meaning that, instead of just dropping a check presenter with "I'll take this when you're ready" or a simple "Thank you," we asked our servers to point out and briefly speak about the comment cards. For example, they could say something like, "Thank you for dining with us tonight. I'll leave your check right here and I wanted to mention that you will find a few of our guest comment cards enclosed. If you don't mind, we would truly appreciate any feedback you have. Also, there is a spot where you can fill in your birthday or anniversary. We do love celebrations around here and I know that management loves to send out some pretty great promotions. Here are a few pens to use, as we'd love for everyone to fill one out!"

We weren't asking our servers to read the form out loud to our guests. We simply wanted them to highlight that they were there and that we took our customers' feedback seriously. Sometimes all you need to do is mention something and it'll get done. As a matter of fact, many of our servers told me that when they mentioned the cards to their tables, more than 90% of the guests filled them out. When they did not get the chance to mention the cards, less than 50% filled them out. Now that is the power of suggestion at work.

And notice how we didn't commit to telling our guests exactly what the promotion would be? Nor did we guarantee there would even be one. Our servers simply suggested that celebrations are important to management and that they liked promotions. This approach opens the door and gets the guest interested, but there is zero commitment. I mention this because some of the feedback I have received when I talk about this marketing tactic with clients is that they are afraid to commit to executing such a marketing strategy every month. They may feel they are too busy, or maybe they decide that they don't want people celebrating at their restaurant—odd, but possible, I suppose. This concern assumes that each guest who fills out the comment card is waiting by the mailbox for their birthday dinner promotion. And wouldn't it be a good thing if they were? It would mean that your restaurant was on their minds. But the reality is, that's probably not the case. For one, the guest probably forgot all about filling out the comment card the minute they left your restaurant, and two, you didn't commit to anything. You simply suggested some festive possibilities. Plus, this is a great way for a guest to complete their experience at your restaurant, knowing that you care about them, their experience, and that you want them to come back.

So now you have trained your service staff on the importance of these cards and how to encourage guests to fill them out. This should result in many guests filling these out during each service. And if you really want to up the ante on these, you can create a contest among the service staff. Maybe whoever collects the most completed comment cards wins a free drink or dessert or small gift certificate that they can use or give away as a gift; you decide what works best for you and your team.

With a trained, incentivized staff ready to knock it out of the park, you could end a busy shift with fifty or maybe even a hundred completed comment cards! More if you're a bigger restaurant, less if you're smaller, but just know that each of these completed cards is gold. It's money in your hands. Here's what happens next…

AN EASY, HOMEGROWN DATABASE IS MONEY IN THE BANK

THIS MAY SOUND A LITTLE old-school—when I implemented this it was the early 2000s, so maybe it *is* old-school—but each time I collected a decent amount of completed comment cards, I set aside some time to enter them into a spreadsheet. I created an Excel workbook with twelve worksheets, one for each month of the year. Within each worksheet, I had a column for each field of data that I collected: name, address, email, birthday, anniversary, favorite menu item, favorite beverage item, etc. It looked something like this:

Name	Street Address	City / Town	State	Zip	Email	Birthday	Anniversary	Fave Menu Item	Fave Bev Item

Depending on how many cards we received, it might take me fifteen to thirty minutes a couple times each week to enter them. These worksheets became our internal CRM (customer relationship management) system, our homegrown database. Also, during slower times, we had our host or another staff member add this information to our reservation software (OpenTable). You can download a sample of this worksheet by going to www.profitfirst4restaurants.com and click on "Tools."

At that time, OpenTable was beginning to develop templated emails that you could send directly through their system, so it made sense to keep that system updated as well. OpenTable is a digital marketing platform, mainly via email. So we did need a separate database—the worksheets—for our snail-mail marketing efforts, but we made them as simple, easy, and user-friendly as possible. This is key. There are many, many different kinds of database software out there, but they all have bells, whistles, and learning curves that you may just not need or have time for. And if you believe that a "good business owner" *would* purchase a fancy CRM database so you buy one and then don't have the time to learn the system, guess what? You just spent a ton of money on something you'll never use, so your marketing won't get done. I've said this before and I'll say it again: keep it simple and get fancy later, but only if you must.

After we entered the information into our homegrown database, we could sort this data any way we wanted. The first thing we did was sort by birthday month and create mailing labels for the following month. Next, we stuck the labels onto letter-size envelopes to get our birthday promotion started. (If you are a small restaurant and prefer more of a personal touch, you could handwrite these envelopes instead of printing labels.) For example, in the last week of June, we created the mailing labels for all the July birthdays. We decided which offer we wanted to promote for that month and printed up the same number of birthday promotions that we had labels for on regular letter-size paper that we printed on our office printer. Then we simply folded the letters, stuffed each labeled envelope with a birthday candle and a letter, added stamps, and mailed the envelopes. Done.

WHAT GETS MEASURED MAKES YOU MONEY

We tested all kinds of promotions. One month, we offered to buy guests a dessert; another month, we offered to buy them an appetizer. We also offered to buy one entrée with the purchase of another, or a percentage discount, or a dollar amount discount—over the years, we tried all the different tactics. Also, we were very clear on our offers that they expired on the last day of that month. After all, these were birthday promotions, and birthdays are generally celebrated within the month they occur. So to stay true to that spirit as well create some urgency, we were not shy about clearly stating when each offer expired. But even more importantly, we *measured* each offer to determine which yielded the best results.

Let's say for our July birthday promotion, we decided to go with "Choose Any Birthday Dessert on Us!" At the bottom of the promotion (the letter), in the fine print, we told the recipient to bring in the letter to redeem the offer. When the guest came in and handed the letter to their server or bartender, that employee attached it to the customer's final check when closing out for the night. This became part of the servers' and bartenders' "checking out" process and it only took them a few extra minutes at the end of each shift. All they needed to do was separate out any promotions they received for that shift and make sure the appropriate guest checks were attached.

As I collected these throughout the month, I added specific data into a second spreadsheet that I created in Excel titled "Measured Marketing." This spreadsheet was even simpler as I didn't need to capture all the comment card information. Here's what we collected in our "Measured Marketing" spreadsheet. Plus, you can download a sample of this worksheet by going to www.profitfirst4restaurants.com and click on "Tools."

July Birthday Promotion — Free Dessert				
Total Check Amount				
Date	# of Guests	Less Tax	Discount Amount	Net Check
6 Jul	2	$ 78.00	$ 8.00	$ 70.00
6 Jul	3	$ 92.00	$ 8.00	$ 84.00
7 Jul	4	$ 125.00	$ 8.00	$ 117.00
8 Jul	2	$ 110.00	$ 16.00	$ 94.00
Total Monthly Promo	11	$ 405.00	$ 40.00	$ 365.00

You can make this spreadsheet as simple or as fancy as you would like. I liked to keep track of the individual promotion; the month during which I ran the promotion (which was the name of the actual sheet within this workbook), the date the promo was redeemed, how many people came in for it, the total amount they spent, the total discount applied, and the net amount received. At one point I did get a little fancier and added the cost of the promotion as well. In this case, the cost would include what we spent on the piece of paper, the envelope, the ink on the paper, the mailing label, the birthday candle, and the stamp. But since those are relatively small expenses, it was easy enough to attach a simple one dollar-per-promotion cost to each promo mailed.

The next month, August, was notoriously a slower month for my restaurant. The city tends to empty out quite a bit over the summer and August is a typical vacation month, so it was a slow month every year. I wanted to make the August offer even more enticing to boost sales, so instead of giving guests a free dessert or appetizer, I decided to give them twenty dollars off their check, and without any of the "fine print." They didn't need to spend a certain amount to get that offer, or anything like that. In fact, they could just come in, spend only twenty dollars and still get twenty dollars off. They could leave without spending a dime (except on gratuity).

My partners thought my idea was crazy. I think they imagined that's what everyone would do, and we would just be out hundreds or thousands of dollars without forcing them to commit to spending a certain amount of money. But I was thinking from the guest's point of view rather than the business owner's point of view. I thought simply of what I could receive from a restaurant that would make me want to go there during my birthday month. And because the generous offer of a specific dollar amount off with no strings attached is a rare promotion to find, I thought this would intrigue, and maybe even endear, enough people to come in and bring their friends that we wouldn't lose money. And if I was wrong, we only had to suck it up for that one month because again, we made it very clear on the letter that this offer expired on the last day of the month. And this is where our "Measured Marketing" spreadsheet became really important. As I tracked our August promotion, we could see the results below.

August Birthday Promotion — $20 Off Your Check				
Total Check Amount				
Date	# of Guests	Less Tax	Discount Amount	Net Check
4 Aug	2	$ 80.00	$ 20.00	$ 60.00
5 Aug	4	$ 196.00	$ 20.00	$ 176.00
5 Aug	6	$ 240.00	$ 20.00	$ 220.00
6 Aug	1	$ 35.00	$ 20.00	$ 15.00
7 Aug	2	$ 78.00	$ 20.00	$ 58.00
8 Aug	3	$ 110.00	$ 20.00	$ 90.00
Total Monthly Promo	**18**	**$ 739.00**	**$ 120.00**	**$ 619.00**

Within the first week of the month, we had already produced more revenue than we did the month prior with a smaller offer. And it brought in more people. More people who filled out more comment cards so that we could now market to them for their birthdays or any event. Plus, if we really blew their minds with a tremendous birthday experience, they might make this an annual event and tell all their friends.

Different promotions will work better or worse for different restaurants. You may not be entirely aware of what speaks to your clientele, but if you try different types of promotions and measure them, you will come to find out what works best for you and your guests.

SUMMARY

DON'T BE AFRAID TO TRY new things, to be generous, unique, kind, funny, whoever you want to be to your guests. You don't have to commit to giving them free stuff indefinitely, or ever, if that doesn't feel right to you. Maybe it feels more natural to simply acknowledge their birthday with a card, a text, or even a phone call!

The Savannah Bananas Baseball Team does exactly that. Or they did when I had the opportunity to visit the team, meet with the owner, and get a behind-the-scenes look at how this fantastic organization is run. Every single person who purchases tickets to one of their games receives a thank you phone call from someone in their office. And not a robocall; this is an actual person, an employee or sometimes even the owner, who picks up the phone to simply say, "Thanks! We look forward to seeing you and hope you enjoy the game!" If you have not heard of the Savannah Bananas, I highly recommend that you look them up as their success story is incredible. If possible, absolutely attend a game, too. It will be unlike any baseball game you have ever seen. And did I mention they use Profit First?

Perhaps acknowledging birthdays doesn't jive with your brand at all. If your concept is more stoic, perhaps more of an old-school "boys' club" with steaks, Scotch, and cigars, your marketing will be geared toward those interests instead. That could mean simply announcing a new Scotch you're carrying or a Scotch dinner coming up. Or maybe you offer complimentary cigars on a certain night and can ask a cigar company to come in and even provide the product so they can promote their cigar brand. You do you—just be sure to measure your efforts so that you have meaningful data about what works, what produces results, and what those results look like.

Even though my Bomboa business partners sometimes thought my ideas were bad or crazy, they couldn't argue with me too much since I only tried things for a month at a time. I would try a promotion for a month, measure it, and move on to something else. I did the same with anniversaries and favorite menu items. For example, with our database of guests who reported that sangria was their favorite beverage, you better believe they received a promotion with a beautiful picture of a pitcher of sangria as summer rolled around.

This kind of marketing is very impactful. But without a way to test a promotion, to try it for a specified period and then measure the results, its effectiveness could be anybody's guess. Without measured results, the success of any campaign is up to anyone's interpretation. And no matter what that interpretation is, it's definitely not money in the bank.

Don't be afraid to try something new, to think outside the box. Think like your guests; think about what they would like to see or be offered and then design a promotion around that. Put guardrails around it in case it doesn't work out, but remember, you won't know what works until you try! And you may be quite surprised by what you find.

CONCLUSION

And This Is How I Know You Can Do It

IMAGINE IF IT WERE DIFFERENT.

Imagine if we believed that our industry is the world's most exclusive club, and everybody wants in—the price of entry being the basic requirements of serving joy, making people happy, and providing an experience that everyone will remember and tell all their friends about. The kind of career that doesn't feel like work, it just feels like being. And while you may not get to be a part of the Monday-through-Friday, nine-to-five crowd, you happily forgo that for a greater purpose. After all, what purpose is greater than providing joy?

We have so many amazing tools at our disposal to produce this result. Incredible food, beautiful wines and cocktails, gorgeous dining rooms and bars with music, lighting, and ambience that you just don't get in a home kitchen or dining room. And that's not to mention the people, the staff, who wholeheartedly believe in true hospitality and love what they do so much that it's not even called work; people from all walks of life who come together with different skills and personalities for the same purpose, the same goal at each service—to make people happy.

The passion and creativity are palpable, from the back of the house to the front of the house. There is a soft, electric current in the air as a choreographed performance flows seamlessly through the restaurant, weaving in and out of the kitchen and dining room, wrapping around the tables, the host stand, the bar, and enveloping everyone in its magic.

Can you see it?

Now, imagine that you no longer have to worry about the money.

You've created a working business model and implemented MacDaddy PF Cash, and the money takes care of itself. Every dollar has a job to do and does it, giving you a clear road map for how to run and manage your restaurant. No more guessing what to do next, no more avoiding unpleasant tasks or overdue bills—everything flows as it should.

And no more hoping and praying for multiple Saturday nights. Every night contributes in its own way. Big money, little money, it's all there, it just needed to be managed—and now it is. Your money has direction, and so do you. With the finances under control, your focus becomes, "How can I bring more joy into today?"

What job sounds better than that?

You don't have to struggle to make it in the restaurant business. There is another way, and I hope I opened you up to the idea in this book.

You should feel incredibly proud of yourself. We did a lot. And this probably wasn't easy. Undoing decades of ingrained beliefs that our industry is supposed to be hard and grueling, as though that is the price of entry, takes work. Undoing any belief system is a complex task, one that requires a vulnerability not everyone is willing to explore. But here you are, at the end of this book, because you're no stranger to hard work and vulnerability. Nobody glides through this work unscathed and without feeling. Every day, every shift, every service is a living, breathing entity of its own and it's impossible not to get swept up in it. There are no bystanders. And while it may not be hearts and lungs, we live and breathe this work. It becomes a part of who we are—like a heart, or a lung.

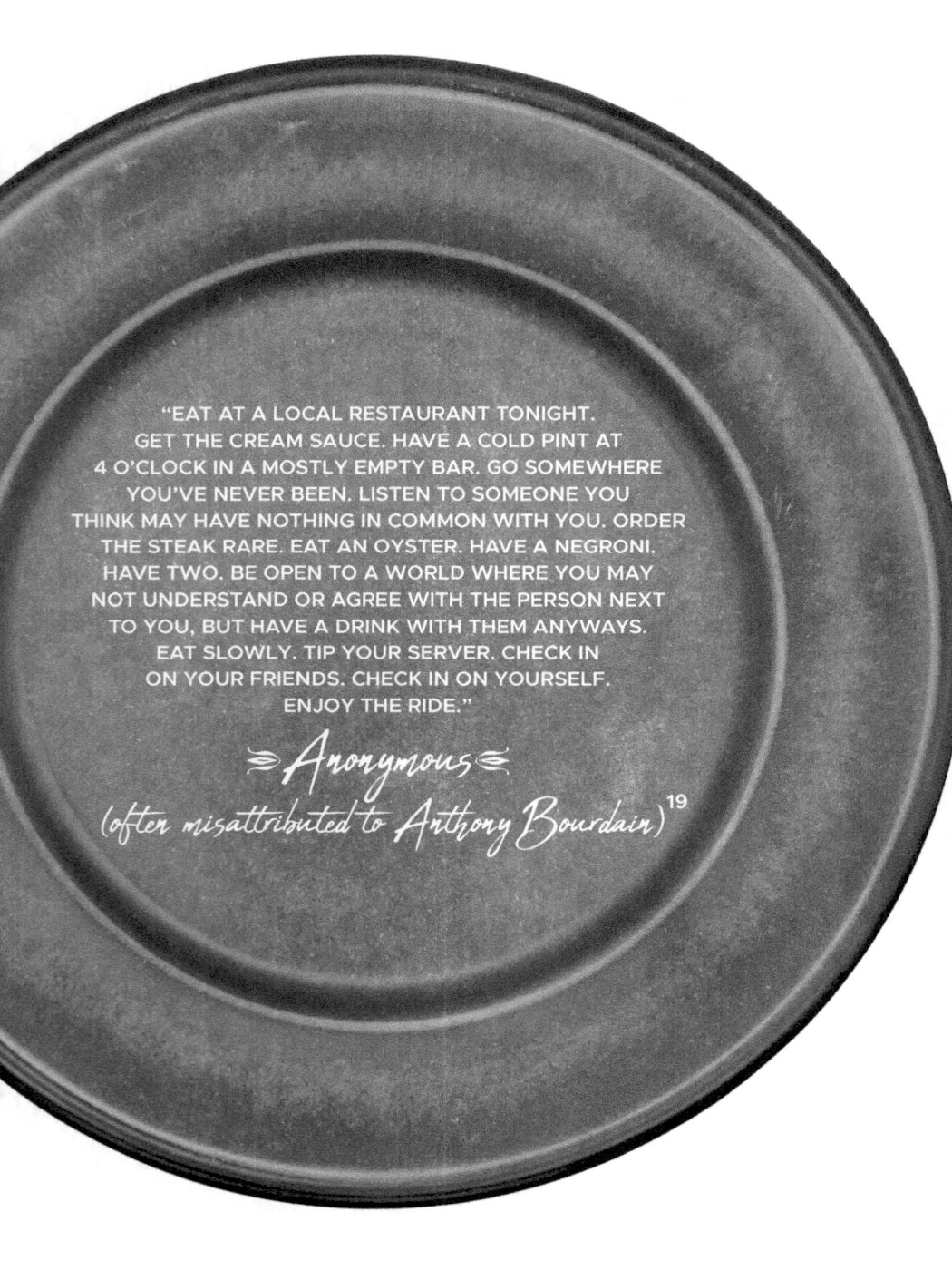

"EAT AT A LOCAL RESTAURANT TONIGHT.
GET THE CREAM SAUCE. HAVE A COLD PINT AT
4 O'CLOCK IN A MOSTLY EMPTY BAR. GO SOMEWHERE
YOU'VE NEVER BEEN. LISTEN TO SOMEONE YOU
THINK MAY HAVE NOTHING IN COMMON WITH YOU. ORDER
THE STEAK RARE. EAT AN OYSTER. HAVE A NEGRONI.
HAVE TWO. BE OPEN TO A WORLD WHERE YOU MAY
NOT UNDERSTAND OR AGREE WITH THE PERSON NEXT
TO YOU, BUT HAVE A DRINK WITH THEM ANYWAYS.
EAT SLOWLY. TIP YOUR SERVER. CHECK IN
ON YOUR FRIENDS. CHECK IN ON YOURSELF.
ENJOY THE RIDE."

Anonymous
(often misattributed to Anthony Bourdain)[19]

GLOSSARY OF TERMS

ALLOCATIONS: ALSO CONSIDERED TRANSFERS, THESE are the amounts of money you move from your Income Account to your other accounts based on your Instant or Profit Assessment CAPs. (Page 52)

Bank Balance Accounting: Using the random balances in your bank accounts on any given day to make decisions for your business. (Page 40)

CAPs: Current allocation percentages which is the current assigned percentage of where the money in your business is currently being allocated among prime costs, profit, owner's pay, owner's taxes, and OPEX. (Page 94)

COGS: Cost of goods sold which generally includes all food and beverage purchases. (Page 72)

Family Meal: A meal that is prepared by the kitchen usually before service and shared among the entire staff preferably during a huddle or pre-shift/pre-service meeting. (Page 244)

GAAP: Generally accepted accounting principles is the US standard in accounting principles. (Page 34)

Huddle: A team meeting that usually takes place before service. (Page 244)

Instant Assessment: A "snapshot" of where your money has historically been going, i.e., to COGS, labor, profit, owner's pay, owner's tax, and OPEX. (Page 66)

MacDaddy PF Cash: The Profit First Cash Management System for restaurants. (Page 69)

OPEX: Operational expenses including overhead and other business expenses outside of COGS, labor, owner's pay, and owner's taxes. (Page 51)

Paper Profit: This is the "net income" or "profit" as recorded on a financial statement such as a P&L yet has no correlation to how much money you have in the bank. (Page 35)

Parkinson's Law: Named after the author and historian C. Northcote Parkinson, this law teaches us that work will expand or contract to match the time allotted for it. (Page 32)

Pre-Shift/Pre-Service: This is a team meeting (see "Huddle"). (Page 244)

Prime Cost: Food, beverage, and labor costs for a restaurant. (Page 33)

Profit Assessment: A deeper, more detailed version of an Instant Assessment, usually completed by a certified Profit First Professional. (Page 93)

Profit First: The cash management system for businesses created by Mike Michalowicz (and the title of his bestselling book). (Page 6)

Real Revenue: The money your restaurant earns after it pays its *direct* meals or sales tax obligations and its prime costs for a given period. On some profit and loss reports, real revenue is similar to the "Gross Profit" line item. (Page 79)

TAPs: Target allocation percentages which are assigned percentages for where you want the money to go in your business when it is running at its best. (Page 114)

ENDNOTES

Epigraph

[1] Danny Meyer Quotes. BrainyQuote.com, BrainyMedia Inc, 2023. https://www.brainyquote.com/quotes/danny_meyer_704148, accessed February 15, 2023.

Introduction

[2] Mike Michalowicz, *Profit First* (Boonton, NJ: Obsidian Launch, 2014).

Chapter 1

[3] Thomas Keller, Michael Ruhlman, and Susie Heller, *The French Laundry Cookbook* (New York, NY: Artisan, 1999).

Chapter 2

[4] Michalowicz, *Profit First, p. 39*

[5] Michalowicz, *Profit First, p.27*

[6] Michalowicz, *Profit First, p. 39*

Chapter 3

[7] Michalowicz, *Profit First, p. 103*

Chapter 5

[8] Michalowicz, *Profit First, p. 61*

Chapter 6

[9] Wolfgang Puck Quotes. AZquotes.com. https://www.azquotes.com/quote/825185, accessed February 15, 2023.

Chapter 7

[10] Peter Economy, "17 Anthony Bourdain Quotes on Food, Business, and Life That Will Inspire You," Inc.com, July 22, 2018, https://www.inc.com/peter-economy/17-anthony-bourdain-quotes-on-food-business-life.html#:~:text=%22Luck%20is%20not%20a%20business,somebody%20else%20figure%20it%20out.%22, accessed February 15, 2023.

Chapter 11

[11] Maryn Liles, "100 of the Best Wit-Filled Anthony Bourdain Quotes About Travel, Food & Life," Parade.com, November 14, 2022, https://parade.com/1105403/marynliles/anthony-bourdain-quotes/, accessed February 15, 2023.

[12] Mark Twain Quotes. QuoteTab.com. https://www.quotetab.com/quote/by-mark-twain/a-tax-is-a-fine-for-doing-well-a-fine-is-a-tax-for-doing-wrong, accessed February 15, 2023.

[13] Definition of "audit." Merriam-Webster.com, https://www.merriam-webster.com/dictionary/audit, accessed February 15, 2023.

[14] Definition of "tax fraud." IRS.gov, https://www.irs.gov/irm/part25/irm_25-001-001#:~:text=Tax%20fraud%20is%20often%20defined,fraudulent%20intent., accessed February 15, 2023.

Chapter 12

[15] Samantha Cole, "Why Some of the Most Innovative Leaders Have an Open Door Policy," FastCompany.com, March 4, 2014, https://www.fastcompany.com/3027128/why-some-of-the-most-innovative-leaders-have-an-open-door-policy, accessed February 15, 2023.

[16] Definition of "top off." Merriam-Webster.com, https://www.merriam-webster.com/dictionary/top%20off, accessed February 15, 2023.

17 Tara Parker-Pope, "How to Have Better Family Meals," NYTimes.com, publication date unavailable, https://www.nytimes.com/guides/well/make-most-of-family-table, accessed February 15, 2023.

Chapter 13

18 Mike Michalowicz, *Get Different: Marketing That Can't Be Ignored!* (Edmonton, Alberta, Canada: Portfolio, 2021).

19 Kim LaCapria, "Anthony Bourdain: 'Eat at a Local Restaurant Tonight' Quote," TruthOrFiction.com, February 16, 2022, https://www.truthorfiction.com/anthony-bourdain-eat-at-a-local-restaurant-tonight-quote/, accessed February 15, 2023.

ACKNOWLEDGMENTS

I NEVER WANTED TO WRITE a book. Not even a little. But here's the thing… I have two great loves of my life. Well, more accurately, I have two great loves of my work life and two great loves of my personal or "real" life. I will tell you about the two great loves of my work life first.

If you've read this book, I hope you can sense my love and passion for the restaurant business and hospitality in general. While I do not work directly within that industry anymore, I can still feel intensely how much it means to me and it will forever be in my blood and DNA. This is my first and forever work love.

My second is Profit First. And I realize that may sound silly, but I promise you, once you implement it in your business, it won't sound so silly anymore. Profit First changed my business and my life in ways I could never have imagined or dreamed of.

I honestly believe that there is no other human being on earth who is as passionate as I am about restaurants *and* Profit First. And when you put those two things together, you get *Profit First for Restaurants* by Kasey Anton. Therefore, my first acknowledgment goes to Mike Michalowicz for not only designing and writing *Profit First*, but also for allowing me the opportunity to author this derivative. It has been my great honor and privilege.

Through Mike, I had the pleasure and honor of meeting and working with AJ Harper and Laura Stone of Top Three Book Workshop. I did not even know what a developmental editor was until I met AJ, and now I cannot imagine a book being written without one. And the education and support provided by AJ, her dean of students, Laura Stone, and the author community they have built is unlike anything I have ever known. Their brilliance has had a profound effect on me and most certainly this book.

I am grateful to have been introduced to my copy editor, Zoë Bird, and book designer, CB "Choi" Messer, by AJ and Top Three Book Workshop. Their skills and dedication to their respective crafts are awe-inspiring, and this book would be a whole lot uglier without them.

Words cannot do justice to how incredibly fortunate I am to work with a team of brilliant, kind, and ridiculously hardworking women like the ones at Spark. I cannot imagine anyone being able to work a full-time job while also writing a book, and these wonder women took the reins and allowed me the space and freedom I needed to focus on this more than yearlong project. To Amy, Stephanie, Jackie, Bree, Laura, Curtisha, Mary, Erin, Kristin, and the entire staff: This book is as much yours as it is mine. Thank you.

I also want to acknowledge and thoroughly appreciate those who agreed to read an advance copy of this manuscript and give me truly invaluable feedback that has made this book even better. Kelle O'Connor, Jason Bond, Chris Hensel, Gena

Comenzo, Ellen Minteer, Natalia Levey, Shawn Vandyke, Chris Moran, Matt Lombardo, Efrain Viscarolasaga, Mike Hargrave, and Angela Goodman, I cannot thank you enough for taking the time out of your very busy lives to do this for me and the book. On behalf of all its future readers, I thank you.

Thank you to my business coach, Kelly Ruta, for giving me the tools and confidence I needed to see this through.

Sara A., Tamara, Rachel, Carole, Laura L., and Krista, thank you for cheering me on with such exuberance that I had no choice but to keep going.

Mom, thank you for all you do for me and your unwavering support. I could not do this without you.

And finally, to the two biggest loves of my life, Clyde and Lucybella: You are the reason for everything I do. Follow your passions. Be kind. Be curious. Be 100% you. It will always be more than enough. I love you more than you could ever know.

ABOUT THE AUTHOR

KASEY ANTON LOVES RESTAURANTS. SINCE she was a kid and as far back as she can remember, restaurants and hospitality have been the center of her passion, and working in and with restaurants has formed her career. She got her first job washing dishes—professionally!—at the age of fourteen and quickly moved through almost every experience and position available in a restaurant, including learning how to properly butcher meat. Her years in the front and back of the house taught her everything she needed to know to move all the way up the ranks to general management, and eventually ownership of her own businesses in Boston.

Owning a restaurant became her master class not just in operating food service, but also in what it takes to be a successful entrepreneur. After the birth of her first child, she opened Spark Business Consulting, whose mission is to help clients understand their business model, master their numbers, build the company of their dreams, and ultimately fall in love with their *profitable* business.

Kasey was first introduced to the book *Profit First* by a couple of her clients, purchased the audiobook, and had her life completely remodeled while listening to it on vacation, resting on a chaise lounge overlooking the Atlantic Ocean.

She leapt from her chair to get the Profit First headquarters on the phone and start her certification process, and the rest is life-changing history.

A born-and-raised New Englander, Kasey can often be found at her office, attending her kids' multiple sports events, reading, learning, traveling, and always enjoying the local restaurant scene. Connect with her at www.sparkbusinessconsulting.com or www.kaseyanton.com.

MACDADDY
RESOURCE MENU

For our main hub of information, check out:

www.sparkbusinessconsulting.com

From here, you can learn all about us,
who we are, and what we do.

Learn about the services we offer at:

www.sparkbusinessconsulting.com/services/

Download our blog posts at:

www.sparkbusinessconsulting.com/blog/

Review and purchase some pretty cool products and tools at:

www.sparkbusinessconsulting.myshopify.com/

Get free checklists and guides at:

www.sparkbusinessconsulting.com/spark-gifts

Check out our online courses at:

www.sparkbusinessconsulting.com/resources/

For our restaurants-only division, go to:
www.spark-eats.com/

MacDaddy Office Hours

**Subscribe and join our monthly call,
where you can show up and ask us anything!**

https://sparkbusinessconsulting.teachable.com/p/
monthly-macdaddy-office-calls

A Day with Kasey

**Need a full day, onsite, soup-to-nuts session?
Book "A Day with Kasey" at your place by visiting:**

https://sparkbusinessconsulting.com/a-day-with-kasey/

Profit First for Restaurants Toolkit

**For access to all the tools built for and
mentioned in this book, go to:**

www.profitfirst4restaurants.com and click on "Tools"

Connect with Kasey

**For information about the author,
or to inquire about speaking engagements,
podcast requests, interviews, etc., go to:**

www.kaseyanton.com

Reader Notes